FRANKLIN
America's "Lost State"

NOEL B. GERSON

FRANKLIN
America's "Lost State"

CROWELL-COLLIER PRESS • NEW YORK
COLLIER-MACMILLAN LIMITED • LONDON

PICTURE CREDITS

For
Michele, Margot and Paul

CONTENTS

Chapter 1.

A STATE OF THEIR OWN

THE TROUBLE, which some American frontiersmen regarded as a blessing in disguise, began in 1782, and its basic cause was simple. The United States had just won her independence from Great Britain after a long and grueling war, and, although another year would pass before the peace treaty was signed, Americans prized their freedom so highly that they refused to take orders or accept the authority of fellow citizens who were not residents of their own immediate region, area, or territory.

The situation in the late Eighteenth century was strangely similar to that which arose more than one hundred and fifty years later, when a spirit of nationalism erupted in Africa, and one new nation after another came into being, changing the map and spirit of a continent. Men everywhere want to be their own masters.

Certainly no people were more surprised, at the end of the American War of Independence, than were the residents of the thirteen United States at the developments everywhere on the frontier. Legislators in Massachusetts were astonished when people in its Maine District began to demand the right to organize a state of their own. New Hampshire was stunned by the movement, led by the Green Mountain Boys, who had fought so valiantly for liberty, to create a new state, Vermont. Virginians, perhaps the most sophisticated of Americans, were sympathetic to the clamor of their Kentucky District for statehood.

The problem faced by North Carolina, however, was unique. Her own past had been difficult—she once had been a part of South Carolina, which made her history of domestic self-rule far shorter than that of the majority of her sister states. She was sensitive, too, because so many of her sons had remained loyal to the British Crown and had fought as Tories. Nowhere had a civil war been waged more ferociously and bitterly than within the borders of North Carolina. Generations would pass before anyone would forget that the frightful Battle of King's Mountain has been fought by Americans against Americans.

Now that peace had come and immigrants by the thousands were moving into the plateau farmlands of North Carolina, many of the Patriot heroes of that battle were crossing the Blue Ridge Mountains and establishing new homesteads for themselves in the rugged wilderness. Already three new counties had been formed, Washington, Greene and Sullivan, all named in honor of prominent generals who had led the American forces to freedom.

The war had virtually bankrupted the infant nation,

and North Carolina, where brother had fought so hard against brother, was particularly impoverished. Farmers whose crops and houses had been burned, whose cattle and livestock had been slaughtered and stolen, left the ruins behind. Townsmen whose shops and small businesses had been destroyed saw new hope and new life in the fertile hill country of the West, where the forests of pine and oak and ash were deep, the rivers pure and swift, the game and fish plentiful.

North Carolina regarded this newly settled region as part of her domain. Her borders, like those of the other states, had been specified in the Crown charter issued when she had been a British possession, and in her case the terms were very clear. All territory due west of the mountains, at least as far as the Mississippi River—perhaps all the way to the Pacific Ocean, if the United States should ever expand that far—belonged to her. Nor could she forget that the wilderness was being settled by North Carolinians.

But the men who rode across the passes into the wilderness, some of them alone, some accompanied by their families, had ideas of their own. It was they, not those who remained comfortably at home, who were running the risks and enduring the hardships of life on a raw and lonely frontier. When the Cherokee and other Indian tribes of the frontier attacked them, they defended themselves without help from the North Carolina militia.

They built their own courthouses and schools, made their own roads and established their own constabulary. Not one penny from the North Carolina treasury was spent on them, a fact that was impressed on every newcomer.

Apparently it did not occur to anyone that, inasmuch as the treasury was empty, the older communities of the North Carolina seaboard received no funds, either.

A lack of communications helped to widen the gulf that separated men on both sides of the mountains. Only a few

The men in the wilderness defended themselves without help from North Carolina when they were attacked.

trails cut across the heights of the Blue Ridge chain. Men either rode horseback or walked, and it required weeks of hard travel to go from Wilmington, on the Atlantic Ocean, to the new towns of Jonesboro and Greeneville. The Blue Ridge, a principal subsidiary of the Appalachian Mountains, did more than separate East and West physically. Men on the two sides of the mountains began to think in different ways.

Certainly the hard-bitten, independent men of the West were extraordinary, literally taming the wilderness. Sometimes, in savage battles, they drove out the Indians whose preserves they had moved into, and yet they could be remarkably patient in diplomatic dealings with them. They cleared land, uprooting stumps so they could plant crops, built their homes with their own hands and grew most of the food they needed to sustain life. Their wives and daughters, knowing and caring nothing about current styles, spun cloth and made clothing. The educated donated time and effort to teach school, administer local affairs and sit in judgment on wrongdoers. No one received wages for such work, and the frontiersman would have been insulted had it been suggested to him that his neighbors should pay him. Everyone helped everyone else freely, unstintingly.

The wilderness dweller neither wanted nor expected aid from the outsider. His one demand was that he be allowed to govern himself as he saw fit.

The trouble stemmed from this fiercely independent attitude, as well as from the equally natural belief of those who remained in North Carolina that it was their duty to administer the newly established parts of the state.

In 1782 the state's legislature began to include the land across the mountains in its bills and directives. The men who had crossed the mountains paid no attention and, when taxes were levied on them, refused to pay. After all, the war with Great Britain had been sparked by the insistence of the Thirteen Colonies that they could not and would not be taxed without their consent.

North Carolina soon realized the error of their course of action and provided places in both houses of the legislature for the new districts of the West. The frontiersmen dutifully elected state Senators and Representatives, but quickly discovered they had no real voice in governing themselves. The men who lived east of the mountains stood together, and the wilderness dwellers formed a small minority whose voices were unheeded and whose needs were ignored. It was inevitable, as it was in the outlying regions of Massachusetts, New Hampshire and Virginia, that the frontiersmen under the jurisdiction of North Carolina began to think of breaking away and setting up their own state.

Had there been a strong national government, perhaps the rights of the frontiersmen might have been better guaranteed and protected. But, from the outbreak of the war against Great Britain in 1775, until five years after its conclusion, the country functioned as the "Confederation of the United States." Each of the thirteen states was supreme, a law unto itself. The ineffective Continental Congress, which had been hampered by the lack of powers granted to it by the jealous states, had been perpetuated and was powerless to intervene on behalf of any group of citizens. Not until 1787 would the Constitutional Convention meet to draw up plans for a new type of government, and not until 1789 would the new Federal Government, with its strong executive, legislative and judicial branches, be established.

Therefore, in 1782, North Carolina could do as she

John Sevier.

pleased in ruling "her territory," or so her legislators believed. They failed to take into account the nature of the Westerners.

The most prominent leader of the men who had crossed the mountains was the military hero of the Battle of Kings Mountain; John Sevier, who pronounced his name Sev-EER. Self-educated, he had served as an officer in the brigade of General Francis Marion and had learned the lessons of guerrilla warfare so well that, when applying them in a campaign against the Cherokee, he had won an overwhelming victory. The climactic battle of the brief campaign had been fought near the banks of the Nolichucky River, so it was almost inevitable that Sevier should be called "Nolichucky Jack" by virtually everyone who lived west of the mountains.

He held a commission as a Colonel in the North Carolina militia, but his followers, many of them King's Mountain veterans, usually referred to him as "General," and he made no protest. Vain, obstinate and quick-tempered, he was also a man of great courage, foresight and ability. He had a natural talent for leadership, most people instinctively trusted him, and he was generally recognized as the first citizen of the Cumberland, as North Carolina's district across the Blue Ridge chain was known.

One of his closest associates in both war and peace was Colonel Arthur Campbell, a brother-in-law of Virginia's distinguished Governor Patrick Henry. Campbell, who had won renown in the war against the British, owned one of the largest farms in the Cumberland and was making experiments to determine what crops produced the biggest yield. Austere in appearance and in manner, Colonel Campbell became violent when defending the cause of liberty, which he held sacred. Everyone in the area knew that his anger would be aroused and he would become the permanent enemy of anyone who tried to curb personal freedoms.

David Campbell, the younger brother of the Colonel, was known to everyone in the Cumberland as "the Judge." He was an attorney who had served on General George Washington's personal staff as a legal adviser, with the rank of Major. He knew that no area could prosper unless law and order were maintained. Since North Carolina had not assigned any judges to sit in courts in the western counties or, for that matter, established any judicial system there, "Judge" Campbell dispensed justice.

He was given firm support by the other leaders and the majority of frontier dwellers, and jails were built in the two principal towns of the Cumberland—Jonesboro and Greeneville. When Knoxville, a little farther to the West, began to flourish a few years later, it, too, had a courthouse and a jail.

One of the younger frontiersmen rising to prominence was Stockley Donelson, later to become the brother-in-law and intimate friend of President Andrew Jackson, who himself migrated to the lands across the mountains a few years later. "Stockley," John Sevier once said, "is so blamed independent that he won't shoot a buck if I point out the animal to him. I've never seen him lose his temper, but he's driven at least four bullies out of the Cumberland, with no help from anyone. Come to think of it, he'd be insulted if anyone even suggested to him that he might need help."

The most retiring, least communicative of the Cumberland's prominent citizens was William Cocke, who was regarded with awe by everyone. Cocke, who lived alone, deep in the forests in a cabin he had built himself, wore leather shirts, trousers and moccasins, shot his own game and did all of his own cooking. He had been the first man to cross the mountains and take up permanent residence in the area, and he knew every hill, every valley, every stream. His friends became furious when he was called "the Daniel Boone of the Cumberland," and they insisted, instead, that Boone was "the Bill Cocke of Kentucky."

Cocke's devotion to liberty was almost fanatical, and, when relations between the West and North Carolina deteriorated, representatives of the state took care to avoid him. He was a superb marksman, at home with all firearms but partial to his long rifle, the universal weapon of the district. It was said he could slice a leaf from a tree with a knife thrown a distance of one hundred paces, but he laughed at the statement, calling it an exaggeration. "I don't reckon I could throw a knife accurately more than seventy to eighty paces," he declared.

It is astonishing that the shy, silent Cocke emerged spectacularly from his shell when the need arose. He began the study of law at the age of thirty-six, was admitted to the bar two years later in 1782 and went on to a brilliant career as a legislator. Eventually he was a principal framer of the Tennessee Constitution, served twelve years in the United States Senate and subsequently became a distinguished jurist. The most amazing aspect of his transformation is that he became the most effective public speaker of his day.

"The defense of freedom," he said many times, "has made me articulate."

Others, among them Landon Carter, James White, Joseph Hardin and Gilbert Christian, rose to prominence as leaders of the Cumberland in its attempt to break free of the shackles of North Carolina. Few of them were as colorful as the Reverend Samuel Houston, whose namesake and nephew became Governor of Tennessee, President of the Republic of Texas, then United States Senator and Governor of Texas.

Perhaps the best educated of the district's leaders, the Reverend Houston had volunteered in the war against the British as a private and had served long and honorably. An exceptionally tall, broad-shouldered man, Houston "rode the circuit," traveling constantly from one small wilderness community to another in order to hold religious services. His manner was dignified, but he was considered somewhat eccentric, because he loved to wear unorthodox clothes, often sporting a broad-brimmed beaver hat and draping a bright blanket over his shoulders.

On one occasion several of his friends protested that he was taking unnecessary chances, making himself vulnerable to attack by bands of Cherokee and Choctaw warriors roaming the forests through which he rode. The Indians, deeply resenting the settlement of lands they considered their own, conducted a steady campaign of terror against the intruders, and a man wrapped in a scarlet blanket was calling attention to himself.

The Reverend Houston's booming laugh echoed across the nearby hills. "Gentlemen," he said, "I place my faith in the Lord, so I know that no harm will come to me. Besides, I carry a rifle and a brace of pistols, and no one, not even Bill Cocke or Jack Sevier, is a better shot than I am. The savages know it, so they'll leave me alone."

All these men of differing temperaments and vocations were drawn together by their mutual, fierce love of liberty —their unyielding demand that they be permitted to govern themselves. By 1782 thousands of settlers were moving into the Cumberland, and the frontier was pushing steadily westward. In fact, some of the residents had already left, thinking the area too "crowded," and during 1779 and 1780 James Robertson had led a party through almost impenetrable forests to the Cumberland River, where he had established a new community called Nashville.

The Confederation Congress was well aware of the mounting tension between the states and the new settlements of the West and sympathized with the pioneers. A motion offered by Congressman Joseph Jones and seconded by Congressman James Madison, who was later to become President of the United States, was passed by an overwhelming vote. It specified that "in case the recommendations to the states of Virginia, North Carolina and Georgia to cede to the United States a portion of their unappropriated western territory shall be complied with, the territory so ceded shall be laid out in separate states at such times and in such manner as Congress shall hereafter direct."

The resolution was only a recommendation, not a directive, since Congress had no power to take matters into its own hands, and the sovereign states of Virginia, North Carolina and Georgia ignored it.

Agitation by the frontiersmen for equality was so strong that other resolutions were passed by Congress, one of the most important being a measure that a majority of delegates heartily approved in the spring of 1782. Designed in part to placate the wilderness dwellers, in part to persuade the seaboard states to release their claims on the territories beyond the mountains, it provided that all new states would adopt a democratic form of government. Spelling out its invitation to the West, the measure specified that new states would become members of the Union and "have the same rights of sovereignty, freedom and independence as the other states." The door was open.

But the North Carolina legislature slammed it shut again, member after member condemning the Confederation Congress for "interfering in matters that are beyond the scope of its authority and none of its concern," as one representative declared. Virginia and Georgia reacted similarly.

Until that time the majority of citizens in the West had not shown much interest in separate statehood. Men who had been conquering the wilderness had been too busy for politics and, ever-optimistic, had assumed they would be treated fairly. Now they bristled. No one, anywhere, could give orders to a frontiersman, to whom liberty was precious. Even those who had been content to remain under the jurisdiction of North Carolina or Virginia were outraged and began to think seriously of forming their own government.

The first to draw up a specific plan was Colonel Arthur Campbell, who said, "The established states have challenged us by balancing a chip on their collective shoulder. We must knock it off."

Unfortunately, the scheme he devised was too ambitious and thoroughly unrealistic. He envisaged the entire West banding together in one huge state, but he quickly learned that others did not feel as he did. The Cumberland and Kentucky had no desire to merge, and residents of the Ohio Valley wanted nothing to do with either. Campbell drew up his first plan in May or June, 1782, and by September revised it, addressing himself only to his fellow Cumberland dwellers.

He and John Sevier were close friends, having served together in the war against the British, so it is reasonable to assume that Sevier read Campbell's plan. The man who would become the undisputed leader of the Cumberland made no comment in writing, however, so his precise, immediate reaction is not known. In view of what followed, he probably agreed with every word.

In any event, Campbell appeared confident that he had the support of his neighbors and sent his plan to the Confederation Congress in the form of a petition, requesting that the Cumberland be allowed to separate from

North Carolina and form a state of its own. Either by design or a remarkable coincidence, Congress more or less simultaneously received a similar petition from a number of Kentucky residents who wanted to separate from Virginia.

Members of the Congressional delegations of the two seaboard states were loudly indignant, and the legislatures were furious. Only a few men, among them Thomas Jefferson of Virginia, the principal author of the Declaration of Independence, who later became the third President of the United States, understood the hopes of the West and supported them. Jefferson had grown to manhood in what had then been a frontier district, so he knew how highly the wilderness men prized the principles of liberty.

Governor Alexander Martin of North Carolina responded to Campbell's petition with the surface calm of a politician who, if he could help it, had no intention of being maneuvered into a corner. He issued a long proclamation, a soothing document that assured North Carolina's citizens on both sides of the mountains that all was well within the expanding, ill-defined borders of the sovereign state.

"The spirit of our government is so moderate," he said, "and the general disposition of our western inhabitants is so good that our subjects will be the last to riot."

For more than six months the Governor's tax collectors had been complaining that they had been forced to flee the wrath of the Westerners. Members of the North Carolina militia who lived on the far side of the mountains ignored calls summoning them to active military duty, and few men in the Cumberland bothered to answer even the most urgent official state correspondence. Since Governor Martin knew of all these problems, it is obvious that he was bluffing.

 *Chapter 2.*

"WE STAND ON OUR
OWN FEET"

PERHAPS THE MOST SIGNIFICANT aspect of the Cumberland's desire for separate statehood is that the movement in its behalf was spontaneous. Years later, on the floor of the United States Senate, William Cocke tried to explain this sentiment. "No one wrote pamphlets urging our people to form their own government," he said, "and no one bothered to make speeches. We held meetings only when we thought the Indians might attack, and no one could afford the waste of hours spent in the saddle, riding through unmarked woods just to hear what he already believed. It was enough that we thought we were being treated unfairly. We stood together because it never crossed our minds to do otherwise."

Ironically, the residents of the Cumberland united to oppose North Carolina in 1783, the year that the United

States and Great Britain finally signed the formal peace treaty that granted Americans their independence. Frontier wits lost no opportunity to draw parallels that would let the whole country know how wilderness men felt, and the Reverend Houston was applauded as the author of the year's most popular sally. "Scratch a Cumberlander," he said, "and you'll find a Patriot. But you wouldn't dare scratch somebody across the mountains for fear of turning up a British Redcoat."

Stockley Donelson, expressing himself for the first time on the subject, saw no humor in the situation. "North Carolina will take all she can from us while giving nothing in return. Clearly we must take care of ourselves."

Governor Martin, watching the rising tide of sentiment on the far side of the Blue Ridge peaks, expressed his own alarm in a confidential letter to a member of North Carolina's Confederation Congress delegation. "It would not surprise me," he wrote, "if the citizens of the new counties, which now number five and continue to grow, resort to armed insurrection in order to obtain their freedom from us. I deplore their inconsistency. They affirm their fealty to North Carolina before leaving the older parts of the state, and at that time they still recognize the validity of the state's claim to her western lands. Let them but spend three months in a new homestead, however, and these loyalties are cast aside. I sometimes wonder whether there is some quality in the very air of the western counties that breeds disaffection. No matter. Let them fulminate, we will not relinquish that which rightfully belongs to us."

The issue was joined.

The breach was not yet final, though, and might have

been healed had extraordinary interest in the entire West not been aroused in the spring of 1783, particularly in North Carolina and her frontier districts. Since no one had ever known the state's precise boundaries in the West, the Governor had appointed a special commission to make a survey. Now, after a year of work—and just as the controversy between the older portion of the state and the Cumberland began to boil—the commission made its report.

Agreement had been reached with Virginia on the demarcation line separating the Kentucky and Cumberland Districts, and the report offered no surprises in this area. But the Cumberland's southern boundary, adjacent to lands claimed by Georgia, always had been vague. The commission settled the issue—at least to its own satisfaction and at the expense of Georgia—by laying claim on North Carolina's behalf to all of the lands within what is known as the "great bend" of the Tennessee River. (The border dispute raged for years, and a portion of the territory in question is now located in northern Alabama.)

The report included glowing descriptions of what the commissioners called "the most fertile, the most beautiful, and potentially the most productive river valleys in the world." Men on both sides of the mountains took notice, and the interest displayed in the eastern portions of North Carolina was particularly keen.

The entire United States was suffering from a financial recession, caused partly by the ravages of the recent war and by the inability of the Confederation Congress to establish a strong national currency. North Carolina, which had no large cities and virtually no industries, was harder hit than most of her sister states. Her farmers, unable to obtain hard cash in return for their produce, were near ruin.

In the late spring of 1783 they began a mass flight to the rich river valleys on the far side of the mountains. Whole families packed their belongings, took their few livestock with them and made the long march to the "Promised Land" in the wilderness. The exodus was so great that members of the North Carolina legislature became alarmed. Whole communities turned into ghost towns, and entire counties were abandoned.

Then, the moment the departing citizens settled on new land that cost them nothing, they refused to accept the jurisdiction of North Carolina. Sometimes loudly, often silently, but always stubbornly, they refused to pay taxes to a state that afforded them no protection from the hazards of the wilderness, built them no roads, hospitals or schools and established neither courts nor a law enforcement system. Like those who had come before them, the pioneers discovered they could depend only on themselves and their neighbors.

Land-promoting companies sprang into being, and the already established settlers, among them Donelson and Sevier, William Blount and Edward Martin, encouraged more and more men to migrate across the mountains. Sevier was now committed to a new future for the area and wrote to Colonel Campbell, "Our most loyal supporters are those who have just arrived and are still clearing their land. They have said a final farewell to North Carolina, and they clamor for the formation of a new state." There was no need for him to add that he and his friends had become active in the instigation of that clamor. Prior to 1783 Sevier's political ambitions had been modest, but now he was beginning to picture the outlines of his destiny and liked what he saw.

Governor Martin was shocked and dismayed by the unexpected developments. "The older portions of the state," he wrote in a special message to the North Carolina legislature, "are being denuded of people. Immediate steps must be taken to insure that our citizens remain subjects of the state."

The legislature, however, was powerless. It could appoint judges, but had no funds to pay their salaries. It could name law enforcement officers, but no one would accept without a guaranteed wage. It had no money to erect the jails, schools and other public buildings that the new residents of the West demanded as their due. And no inducements could persuade men to become tax collectors in the West, where settlers did not hesitate to fire their long rifles, with great accuracy, at strangers they disliked.

Within the limitations it could control, North Carolina did what it could for its Western District. A bill was passed by the legislature and signed by Governor Martin authorizing the raising of a militia regiment in the territory. John Sevier was appointed its commander, and commissions as senior officers were granted to other Cumberland men who had distinguished themselves in the war.

The legislature sent a committee composed of a select group of its own members to the area for the purpose of making a general survey to determine the West's needs, but the mission had unexpected repercussions when three of the five members were so impressed that they decided to

The settlers refused to pay taxes to North Carolina.

move to the Cumberland themselves. An attempt also was made to survey the area so roads could be built where they were most needed, but the project was a dismal failure, and with good reason.

The land fever was so great that experienced, professional land surveyors were much in demand and doubled, sometimes tripled their usual fees. The entire region, as far west as the bluffs overlooking the Mississippi River on which the city of Memphis eventually grew, was carefully mapped, with particular attention paid to water resources, the fertility of the soil, the game in the region and the quality of the timber. These surveyors were working for private groups of Cumberland citizens who were laying claims to large parcels of land, so only the very young were free to accept employment from North Carolina. They, knowing little of what was required of them, bungled their assignment so badly that they earned the contempt of the Cumberland and made the split between North Carolina and her territory wider.

An unfortunate by-product of the land-fever race was the settlers' ruthless treatment of the Indians—an attitude as old as the oldest seaboard communites and on that would persist through the better part of the Nineteenth century as the United States continued to expand westward. North Carolina's treaties with the large, powerful Cherokee Nation and the smaller but warlike Choctaw were ignored, and many hundreds of thousands of acres that had been granted to the Indians as preserves were either occupied or marked for future settlement. Even the docile, peace-loving Chickasaw tribe became incensed when its rights were violated.

Warriors of the three nations felt they had no choice

and began campaigns of scalping, burning, looting and killing in an attempt to drive the settlers out. The frontiersmen met force with force, and John Sevier's regiment of unpaid volunteers was kept busy fighting the beleaguered tribes. According to Nolichucky Jack's own account, he himself took part in more than ninety campaigns and expeditions against the Indians in the decade beginning in 1780. He was inclined to stretch the truth on occasion for the sake of making a better story, but the figure may not be far off the mark. Even though no accurate records of such expeditions were kept during the period (warfare against the Indians being considered a normal and natural way of life), at least some facts are known about sixty-five campaigns in which Sevier participated.

General Richard Caswell, who had fought in the wilderness against the British, succeeded Martin as Governor of North Carolina, and the frontiersmen believed him more sympathetic to their cause. They had other, equally important reasons for hoping that the climate was changing, chief among them being the fact that Virginia ceded her Kentucky District to the national government, which virtually insured the eventual emergence of Kentucky as a state in her own right. What the Cumberland dwellers failed to take into account was that many of Virginia's leaders were thoroughly familiar with the problems of the wilderness and sympathized with the settlers' aspirations. The two most powerful Governors of Virginia since the United States had declared her independence, Patrick Henry and Thomas Jefferson, had lived on the frontier themselves. General George Washington, the American wartime com-

mander-in-chief who was the most influential man in the
country, lived on the Virginia seaboard, but had been a
wilderness surveyor in his youth and had been a hero of a
long march deep into Pennsylvania in the last of the wars
against the French and the Indians.

There were no comparable giants in North Carolina, although many of her most competent, conscientious citizens
were prominent in the government. In addition to Caswell

William Blount.

there was Thomas Banbury, who was Speaker of the House. In the legislature were William Hooper, a signer of the Declaration of Independence, who had later served in the Continental Congress, and Samuel Johnston, who subsequently became Governor. Alexander Mebane, Thomas Person and William Lenoir were men of proven ability, as were John Hay and John Ashe. Of these leaders, unfortunately, only Caswell had ever paid a single visit to the West.

An act to cede the lands across the mountains to the national government was introduced in the legislature by William Blount, a Cumberlander, but it met strong, unyielding opposition. At a critical time in 1784 Martin became Governor again, and Caswell stepped down to the post of President of the State Senate, a place of honor with little power.

The debate became increasingly bitter, and so many amendments were added to the cession bill that it became virtually worthless. In fact, Landon Carter and Elijah Robertson, the leaders of the delegation from the Cumberland, were forced to oppose the measure. In the spring of 1784 the bill passed the legislature, over the protests of a far-seeing minority, and was signed into law by Governor Martin. The Cumberland, in theory, one day would become a national territory like Kentucky and would be free to pursue its own goal of statehood. For all practical purposes, however, the bill contained so many conditions, so many subtle, hidden clauses, that the territory would remain a part of North Carolina for as long a period into the future as men could envisage.

It must be remembered that the residents of the Cumberland long had known self-government. While most had lived in North Carolina, some had come to the territory from Virginia and Georgia, and relatively small numbers had migrated from Pennsylvania and Delaware, New York and Connecticut. Ever since 1775 these men and their fathers had obeyed only the laws made by their own elected representatives in their own state legislatures.

Consequently the indignation that swept through the Cumberland was spontaneous when men heard the news of the cession bill. Sevier, Colonel Campbell and their friends were not reluctant to fan the flames of anger. By now Campbell was considered the "father of Cumberland independence," and the ambitions of Sevier, which had been growing rapidly, appeared to be within reach.

Campbell was the moving spirit in a campaign to call a convention of Cumberland citizens for the purpose of considering whether the territory should accept the North Carolina cession or take "other steps," as Campbell vaguely said in letters he sent to virtually everyone he knew. He did not specify the nature of these "others steps," and there was no need to spell out his meaning. Wilderness men realized that the real purpose of holding a convention was to determine how and when the territory would declare itself free of North Carolina and, in defiance of Governor Martin and his legislature, set up a free and independent state that would then apply for admission to the Union.

The militia regiment and two separate battalions that had also been formed provided the nucleus of the delegates to the convention. Two members of each company were elected as representatives to a preliminary convention in the locality they represented, and these preliminary conventions established the rules to be used in the election of delegates to the principal convention. The militiamen, almost without exception, were devoted to the cause of Cumberland independence, so it is not surprising that, through the clever process of screening, few men who favored a maintenance of the relationship with North Carolina were elected.

Here and there in the Cumberland District were a handful of men who wanted to keep the territory under the control of the mother state. But they were in such a distinct minority that at no time, then or later, was their collective voice significant. It well may be that anyone opposed to the District's independence kept a discreet silence. Frontiersmen were as passionate in their convictions as they were strong-willed, and it was always possible that those who opposed the will of the majority might be physically intimidated by their neighbors. Democracy had not been made a perfect instrument of the people's will in frontier lands, and small minorities often found it wise not to express their beliefs.

On August 23, 1784, delegates from the three oldest counties and representatives from the newer areas, which were called counties but had not yet formally defined their boundaries, gathered at Jonesboro. There is no precise figure on the number in attendance; according to some reports there were approximately fifty delegates there, but others have written that the total was closer to one hundred. John Sevier and Landon Carter were elected president and secretary, respectively, both by acclamation.

No minutes or other formal record of what took place at the convention has survived, and the best account of what transpired is to be found in a memorandum written by the

Reverend Houston, who was a delegate. Apparently the members lost no time attending to the major business that had brought them together. After several men had made brief speeches advocating separation, a delegate unidentified for posterity offered a resolution declaring that the West was independent of North Carolina.

There was no discussion, and the measure was adopted by an enthusiastic, unanimous vote.

William Cocke made the principal speech, outlining a future for the Cumberland so bright with promise that he was interrupted repeatedly by thunderous applause. The delegates were listening to what they wanted to hear.

There were complications, however, that forced the leaders to tread cautiously. No precedent existed for the steps the territory was taking; never before had an appendix to a state declared itself free and readied itself to request a place at the council table of equal states, which included its parent. There was no guide for the convention to follow, everyone knew that North Carolina would oppose the action, and it was impossible to guess how the other states would react. It was time the frontiersmen showed they could be diplomats, too.

Even though the Confederation Congress was weak and lacking in prestige, it was the only governmental body in which all thirteen states were represented. So the convention, hoping to win the good will and approval of its members, adopted several resolutions offering the much-maligned Congress lavish praise to which it was unaccustomed. Statehood for the Cumberland depended in large part on the support generated in other parts of the United States.

The convention, its immediate business accomplished, adjourned for a month, but heavy rains, Indian raids and the need to keep a sharp watch for North Carolina tax agents, who were escorted back across the mountain "border," delayed the meeting until November. Then the delegates came together for no more than two confused, trying days, and even the most optimistic were learning that unexpected complications could make the goal of statehood difficult to achieve.

The ostensible reason the delegates returned to their homes so soon was that the North Carolina legislature had just been called into session, and men in the territory wanted to see how the mother state would react to their challenge before they took additional action. This was valid and sensible, but there were other, unpublicized causes of the adjournment that made even the most zealous advocates of independence uneasy.

One was the lack of support for the Cumberland movement in Kentucky. Colonel Robertson was still hoping the two territories would join together to form a single new state and was stunned by the indifference of the Kentuckians to the idea. Since their own road to statehood seemed unobstructed, the men of Kentucky had no desire to accept unnecessary burdens.

An even harsher blow was the refusal of Davidson County, far to the west, to join in the independence movement. Nashville, the principal community of Davidson County, was the fastest-growing town in the territory, and, almost overnight, had become the largest. So the refusal of men there to take part in the venture was a crippling blow.

John Sevier lost his temper when he heard Davidson County had rejected his ambitious scheme. "Nashville," he snapped, "is a nest of traitors." The people of that city never forgave him.

There were two fundamental reasons Davidson County would not take part in the drive to establish a separate state. Certainly men there loved liberty no less than did those in the older counties. But they were separated from Jonesboro and Greeneville by the Cumberland Mountains and a vast stretch of uninhabited forest, and consequently were not in close touch with Sevier, Campbell and their friends. This physical remoteness made them less subject to the attempts of North Carolina to interfere in their affairs. The state's tax collectors never traveled that far, so residents of Nashville avoided many of the burdens imposed on less remote districts.

An even more important reason for Davidson County's "loyalty" to the mother state was economic. Many—perhaps a majority—of the County's property owners were men who had acquired their homesteads under grants given by North Carolina to her militia veterans, the area having been designated by the legislature for that specific purpose. The former North Carolina soldier who had traveled so far across the wilderness to establish his new home knew that, if he disavowed the authority of North Carolina, the document guaranteeing his ownership of one hundred and sixty acres of land in Davidson County would no longer be legal, and he would be reduced to the status of a squatter.

So he had no intention of taking part in the freedom movement initiated by the older parts of the territory.

Nor had he any intention of actively opposing Sevier and Campbell in their efforts to set up a new state. Frontier dwellers believed in minding their own business and not interfering with others, and, to an extent, the people of Davidson sympathized with the attitude of the territory's older counties. As Governor Martin and his associates well knew, any attempt by the state to use force against one part of the territory would unite the entire District overnight.

Not until the situation became much more acute did it finally occur to thinking men in Nashville and the rest of Davidson County that, if a new state came into being between them and North Carolina, it would become almost impossible for them to remain a part of the parent state. Then they would face the choice of joining their neighbors or setting up still another state of their own. For the present, however, they were content to walk alone, hoping the storm clouds would dissipate.

Few North Carolinians showed much foresight, either. Virtually the entire state exploded in righteous wrath when newspapers told them what had happened at the Jonesboro convention in August, 1784. Hotheads in both branches of the legislature wanted to send strong militia units across the mountains to subdue the "rebels," and Governor Martin was relieved that the legislature was not in session. He, at least, knew that men like Sevier, Colonel Campbell and William Cocke would not submit tamely, and that a full-scale civil war would be waged in the rugged hills of the Cumberland.

The aroused citizens of North Carolina were too indignant to let their leaders seek a calm solution of the problem through diplomatic measures. They demanded action, and the election of a new legislature in the early autumn gave them an opportunity to express their feelings in no uncertain terms. Men who either felt the insurgents might be right or who sought compromise were defeated, almost without exception, and a legislature pledged to "teach the Cumberland a lesson" was elected.

The legislature met in October, 1784, and promptly

Frontier dwellers in Davidson feared the loss of their hard-won land.

showed its mood by rescinding the Cession Act. Although that measure would have delayed the independence of the territory for years, perhaps permanently, it had been a token gesture of good will.

The outright repeal of the act was a contemptuous, deliberate blow, however. Judge David Campbell spoke for the entire Cumberland when he said, "North Carolina has struck us in our vital parts with a bayonet."

Virginia, which had worked out her own, similar problem with her Kentucky District in a peaceful, amicable manner, offered her services as a mediator. Governor Martin was willing, but his legislature gave him no choice, both houses passing a joint resolution of rejection worded in such an insulting manner that Virginia was deeply offended.

The net result of this flurry was that Virginia, which ordinarily would have sided with a sister state in the dispute, now took the part of the Cumberland. The state that, with Massachusetts, stood first in prestige everywhere in the United States became the Cumberland's self-appointed spokesman in the Confederation Congress, and in the stormy years that followed unflaggingly defended the territory's cause.

Later the Cumberland would be grateful for Virginia's friendship. At that moment, however, the leaders of the territory were too enraged to appreciate any gestures on their behalf. North Carolina had challenged them, and wilderness men never refused to fight. The Campbell brothers, members of the Hardin family and many others in the Cumberland were intelligent, educated men who realized that the odds against attaining separate statehood were great and that North Carolina's harsh opposition made them greater. But the frontiersmen would not be intimidated.

By the end of October, as soon as news of the North Carolina repeal of the Cession Act reached the Cumberland, the territory's leaders set up a temporary government of their own. The militia regiment and separate battalions were combined into a single brigade under the command of John Sevier, whose friends gave him the rank of Brigadier General. The brigade was directed to "maintain order in our land and prevent its invasion by outsiders." There was no need to identify these outsiders.

Four judicial districts were established, with a judge in each, and David Campbell was named Presiding Justice of a Superior Court that would supervise the activities of lower courts and hear appeals. Plans were made, too, to collect taxes, to prevent any goods made in North Carolina from crossing the border and to seek financial help from other states. But these projects were kept secret for the moment.

The Cumberland's leaders recognized the need to proceed with due process of law. They were totally committed now to the cause of establishing their own state and were determined to make as few mistakes as possible.

 *Chapter 3.*

"FRANKLIN EXISTS"

ON DECEMBER 14, 1784, the elected representatives of the Cumberland's citizens opened a meeting at Jonesboro that came to be called the First Constitutional Convention. There is no complete list of those who attended, but the only building in town large enough to accomodate the entire group was the recently built Presbyterian Church. Sevier became president, and John A. Ramsay was elected secretary.

The session opened on a cheerful note with a report on the prospects of the area, prepared by Cocke and Joseph Hardin and read by the latter in his best oratorical style. It said, in part:

> *To remove the doubts of the scrupulous, to encourage the timid, and to induce all, harmo-*

niously and speedily, to enter into a firm associ-
ation, let the following be considered:

If we should be so happy as to have a sepa-
rate government, vast numbers (of people) from
different quarters, with little encouragement from
our own public, would fill up our frontier, which
would strengthen us, improve agriculture, perfect
manufactures, encourage literature and every
thing truly laudable. The seat of government,
being among ourselves, would tend not only to
keep a circulating medium in gold and silver
among us, but draw it from many individuals liv-
ing in other states, who claim large quantities of
lands that would lie in the bounds of a new state.

Add to the foregoing reasons the many
schemes, as a body, we could execute to draw it
among us, and the sums which many travelers
out of curiosity, and men in public business
would expend among us.

The report went on to cite the Cumberland's grievances
against North Carolina. A recent law taxed land in the
District on the same basis as that in the mother state, even
though property in the Cumberland was worth only one-
fourth as much as that in North Carolina. The state legislature, after opening the door to statehood for the territory, had slammed it shut again.

The resolution ended with a motion establishing a
separate state, to become effective as rapidly as possible.
There was little debate, and the measure was passed by an
overwhelming majority, with only fifteen delegates vot-

Benjamin Franklin was proud to give his name to the new state.

ing against it. A large crowd that had gathered outside the church cheered when they learned the news, and that night bonfires were lighted.

A committee drew up a letter to the most distinguished of Americans, Benjamin Franklin, inviting him to make his home in the new state and requesting permission to name it after him. There appears to have been little discussion of the subject of a name, and the author of the idea to call it Franklin is unknown. In any event, the choice was a popular one. Dr. Franklin had a greater prestige than any other American, both at home and in Europe. He was a diplomat and statesman, a noted philosopher, an inventor of stature and had acquired both fame and wealth as an author, editor, publisher and printer. He often had encouraged the development of frontier settlements and had been active in companies promoting the growth of new regions.

Dr. Franklin's prompt reply was both regretful and encouraging. He had so many interests in Philadelphia, he said, that he could not move elsewhere, particularly at his advanced age. But he was proud to give his name to the new state and wished her people prosperity and peace.

The convention adjourned for Christmas, but the delegates returned a few days later to begin drawing up a temporary constitution. Committees were formed to establish a permanent judiciary, find ways to raise funds for a state treasury and attend to the permanent defense of the new state.

Governor Martin and his successor, Governor-elect Caswell, took immediate and energetic steps, both financial and political, to keep the Cumberland in North Carolina's fold. Under the terms of her treaties with the Cherokee and Chickasaw nations, North Carolina was obliged to provide the tribes with large quantities of beef, pork and corn each year, and it had long been a major source of irritation to Cumberlanders that, although they lived adjacent to the Indians, these supplies always had been purchased within the boundaries of North Carolina.

Now Governor Martin and the Governor-elect promised to buy these foodstuffs from Cumberland farmers, not only in 1785, but in future years as well. So the frontier settlers, who were always short of cash, could earn at least one hundred thousand dollars annually. These purchases would be made, however, only if the Cumberland remained a part of North Carolina.

The political offers were equally tempting. Only Cumberlanders would sit in the law courts of the District, and all other officials in the territory would be men who resided there. John Sevier was offered a commission as a Brigadier General of the North Carolina militia. Even the tax collectors in the District would be Cumberlanders. And, Martin and Caswell declared, they would make every effort to persuade the legislature to pass a new bill ceding the territory to the national government within a reasonable period of time, this guarantee being "irrevocable" once a new act was passed.

The terms were both generous and clever, and many Cumberland men had second thoughts about secession. Among them was Colonel Campbell, who was aware of the many problems a new state faced and who wondered whether it might be wise for the District to postpone its aspirations so the citizens of the region could enjoy immediate, concrete benefits. Even John Sevier hesitated briefly, but William Cocke had no doubts and insisted that the convention continue to meet.

While others debated, Cocke wrote a preface to the proposed state constitution, calling it a "Declaration of Independence." In it he cited all the now familiar reasons for forming a new state and added a new one, the "necessity of maintaining a decent respect."

David Campbell worked with Cocke on the constitution, which was closely modeled on that of North Carolina. It contained a very strong Bill of Rights, guaranteeing individuals personal freedoms, and when this section was read to the assembled delegates, it brought them to their feet, appaluding.

Colonel Campbell went off to North Carolina to test the "true sentiments" of Martin and Caswell and returned with a fresh desire to go ahead with the formation of a new state. Both the old Governor and his successor had made it plain to him that they were unalterably opposed to the secession of the Cumberland. Campbell had asked what would prevent them from repealing a new Cession Act, and their evasive replies convinced him that such an act would be as flimsy and temporary as the earlier one.

The Cumberland leaders no longer hesitated. Sevier, Campbell and the others closed ranks, and the temporary constitution was put into effect. For a period of no less than six months and no more than twelve, the citizens would be given the opportunity to vote on changes, additions and deletions they might want incorporated in a permanent constitution.

The state of Franklin was inching its way into being, but the final step—that of severing relations with North Carolina—had not yet been taken. For all practical purposes the men of the Cumberland had established their separate identity, but their governmental machinery was not yet in completed, functioning shape, and they were in no hurry. For the present, and for some months to come, the area existed in a curious twilight zone and was neither a self-proclaimed state nor a district under the control of an already established state.

Colonel Campbell was the author of a long, persuasive petition sent to the Confederation Congress early in the spring of 1785, requesting that Franklin be admitted to the Union as a state. During this same time he corresponded with a number of Kentucky leaders, urging them to reconsider and join the people of the Cumberland in forming a single new state.

Meanwhile Cocke wrote a barrage of replies to communications, both official and informal, from the authorities of North Carolina. He vigorously refuted their charges that Franklin was acting illegally, and he presented long arguments contending that the men of the Cumberland had the right to set up their own government. Sevier corresponded with Governor Patrick Henry of Virginia, courting his favor, and Judge Campbell wrote a carefully worded letter to Benjamin Franklin in which he expressed the hope that the "godgather" of the new state would protect it against "short-sighted political foes." In brief, everything possible was being done to protect the new state in the battle of words that was certain to take place.

During February, 1785, the individual towns and rural districts of Franklin elected their representatives to the state Assembly, or legislature. The organization of the commonwealth's affairs was so haphazard that there was no one day when all the citizens went to the polls. Each community set its own date, and many voters were forced to spend as long as eight or ten hours in the saddle, riding across rugged hills, in order to reach their polling places.

The members of Franklin's first state Senate and House began to gather in Jonesboro early in March, and, although no town had been designated as the capital, the log cabin community of Jonesboro won the honor simply because the members of the new legislature gathered there.

There was no quorum as yet, so the delegates kept busy by constructing a statehouse, a two-story clapboard building that was the largest edifice west of the Blue Ridge Mountains. Other newly elected members drifted into Jonesboro one by one, and around the middle of March enough were on hand to open the First General Assembly. The proceedings were so informal that the precise date of this historic occasion is unknown.

There is no roster of the Assembly's membership, nor has any record of its voting on various measures been preserved. Like all good frontiersmen, the Franklinites

The largest edifice west of the Blue Ridge Mountains in 1785.

were more concerned with getting things done than with recording their activities for posterity.

John Sevier was elected the first Governor of Franklin. Whether the Assembly voted him into office unanimously, as his friends said, or whether there were other candidates, as his opponents later declared, is a mystery that has never been solved. It was sufficient, at the time, that he was elected. Landon Carter became President of the Senate, and William Cage was made Speaker of the lower chamber, which was called the House of Representatives in some documents and the House of Commons in others.

The Assembly was furiously busy during the last two weeks of March. A judiciary was established, and David Campbell was elected Chief Justice of the Supreme, or Superior Court. Bills were passed "for the promotion of learning" throughout the state, and provisions were made to build schools in every town, village and rural area. Never before had the people of any state shown such interest in education, and one of the legislature's first acts made it mandatory that all boys attend school until their fourteenth birthdays. In Franklin, as elsewhere, no one seemed to care whether girls went to school.

An act was passed establishing a state militia, others formed new counties, and some, urgently needed, established land taxes and granted the Governor the right to appoint tax collectors. It was decided, for the present, to use the paper currency of North Carolina and the foreign coins of gold and silver that were in general circulation elsewhere in the country, the United States not yet having started to mint its own coins.

State bonds were issued for the purpose of raising

revenue, and the bill passed by the legislature for this purpose specified that they were payable in as yet non-exis-
tent "Franklin currency." A commission was named, too,
to design a "great seal" and an "honorable flag" for the
state.

Not until March 31st did the Assembly remember that
the formal ties of the Cumberland with North Carolina
had not yet been broken. This oversight was rectified that
same day by the passage of an act declaring that Franklin
was a free and independent state, sovereign unto itself,
"but subject to the general laws of the United States, to
which Confederation it herewith begs admission."

Governor Sevier signed the measure that same day. According to North Carolina wits, the act did not become law
until April 1st, which, they declared, "makes Franklin the
biggest April Fools' Day jest in all history."

At least ten more days passed before Sevier finally sent
a copy of the bill to North Carolina, giving the document to
a nephew who acted as an official courier. North Carolinians charged that the delay was a deliberate insult, but
they were mistaken. The Governor and Assembly were so
busy that no one had time to make a copy of the document.
Most acts were posted on the front door of the statehouse
for passing citizens to read, and no copies whatever were
made of them.

Bills had to be drawn and passed to establish every state
and county office, from the Attorney General, Treasurer
and Secretary of State to justices of the peace. One of the
most important posts was that of State Surveyor, the precise boundaries not having been determined and some
forest areas not having been thoroughly explored. Stock-

ley Donelson was elected to this position, and, without waiting for the legislature to adjourn, went to work immediately.

Governor Martin of North Carolina still hoped the secessionists could be conciliated and sent a personal representative, Major Samuel Henderson, to Franklin for the purpose. Henderson arrived in Jonesboro in time to see the Assembly in action, and the legislators courteously drew up and passed a resolution thanking North Carolina for past favors, while firmly asserting the intention of the new state to maintain its separate identity "at any cost," adding, "No child asks to be brought into the world, but once it has been born, it exists from that time henceforth. Franklin exists, and regards you with affection, but from a distance."

North Carolina's mood changed from one of conciliation to anger when the resolution was received. It was obvious that Franklin had no intention of working out a compromise satisfactory to everyone and was concerned only with her own interests, so the North Carolinians stiffened. They realized their own standing in the community of states would be lessened if they accepted the secession without active protest, and the leaders closed their ranks. Even those who had sympathized with the ambitions of Franklin felt that the mother state was being insulted.

An extraordinary situation, one unique in the short history of the United States, had arisen. A portion of a state, acting without permission or approval, had declared itself independent and had established its own government. North Carolina citizens felt disgraced and united in an effort to find some way to rebuke Franklin and force its return.

Meanwhile the frontiersmen at Jonesboro ignored the tempest across the border and organized their own campaign for admission to the Union. The Assembly unanimously elected William Cocke to a special position, called Commissioner of the State of Franklin, and directed him to appear before the Confederation Congress to make a formal request for equal membership in the sisterhood of states.

The wilderness dwellers blithely took over other functions of sovereignty, too. Aware that the treaties with the Indian nations of the area had been made by North Carolina, they could not expect the tribes to consider these agreements binding if they themselves had broken away from the parent state. A special commission was formed, with Governor Sevier as chairman, to work out a new treaty with the Cherokee and Choctaw, the most warlike of the tribes. Couriers were sent to the main settlements of both nations, inviting them to a council of peace in Jonesboro.

North Carolina regarded this impertinent disregard of her treaties as the last straw. In an atmosphere of crisis the inauguration of the new Governor was postponed in order to keep the experienced Governor Martin at the helm a little longer. The highest ranking state officials gathered in the temporary capital of New Bern, which they sometimes spelled Newbern, and held a series of urgent conferences behind closed doors.

No minutes of those sessions were ever revealed, but enough is known to gain a general idea of what had happened. A few legislators were so incensed that they wanted to send the militia to Jonesboro and place all officials of Franklin under arrest. Other leaders were alarmed by the suggestion, knowing that the tough frontiersmen would not submit meekly and that an all-out civil war would take place.

"If we intend to invade Franklin," Governor Martin said with somber realism, "we shall have to do a great deal more than make a few token arrests. Do you think that men who fought at Kings Mountain and have engaged in so many Indian campaigns will allow themselves to be made prisoner? If we want to subdue the Cumberland by force, we shall need far more troops than are enlisted in our entire militia. We'll need help from other states!"

Messengers were sent to neighboring states, asking for military assistance if North Carolina decided to use force. Georgia, Virginia and Maryland politely but firmly declined to participate in such a campaign, and only South Carolina reluctantly promised to send troops for an expedition. "Sevier," the South Carolina reply said, "may be a fool. But he and his riflemen don't shoot like fools. It might be necessary to muster all the veterans of the recent war in order to force their surrender."

The North Carolinians had second thoughts, became less belligerent and began to study other methods of trying to cope with the situation. Perhaps, they decided, an appeal to the patriotism of the mountain men might be effective.

The wilderness dwellers were aware of the flurry they had caused, but were undisturbed by it. "We sleep with our rifles beside us in the best of times," Sevier told a visitor from North Carolina. "If we're able to keep hostile Indians at a distance, I don't believe we have much to fear from invaders from North Carolina."

The "invasion," when it took place, consisted of a long barrage of words. A manifesto, drawn up by all of the North Carolina leaders, was signed by Governor Martin and published on April 25, 1785. It was a rambling document that attacked Franklin's legal position, rebuked her citizens for disloyalty and then, in a sudden turnabout, begged them to reconsider their "rash action and return to the embrace of North Carolina."

The official copy of the manifesto was sent to John Sevier, addressing him not as Governor of Franklin, but as a Colonel of the North Carolina militia. The framers of the document made a slip, however, much to the amusement of the Franklinites, and referred to him throughout the paper as Brigadier General Sevier, a rank he had been given by his fellow frontiersmen.

Approximately five thousand copies of the manifesto were published, and copies were sent to every man who had been elected to office in Franklin, to every member of the new state's militia and to other citizens of the Cumberland whose addresses were known.

As his last act in office, Martin summoned the legislature of North Carolina to a special session "for the purpose of dealing with the revolt in the Cumberland." Martin, who had been conciliatory until this time, was now exasperated. Had he remained in office it is possible that a civil war really might have broken out in the late spring or early summer of 1785. His tone in calling his legislature into session was so unyielding that the Franklinites, for the first time, gave serious consideration to the possibility of armed conflict.

Fortunately, however, he gave up the post of North

State of North Carolina

By his Excellency Alexander Martin Esquire, Governor Captain General and Commander in chief of the said State.

To the Inhabitants of the Counties of Washington, Sullevan, and Greene.

A Manifesto.

Whereas I have received Letters from Brigadier General Sevier, under the style and character of Governor; and from Mess.rs Landon Carter and William Cage, as speakers of the Senate and Commons of the State of Franklin; informing me that they with you the Inhabitants of part of the territory late ceded to Congress, had declared themselves independent of the State of North Carolina, and no longer considered themselves under the sovereignty and jurisdiction of the same; stating their reasons for their seperation and revolt; among

74.

The first and last pages of the North Carolina manifesto, which refers to Sevier as "Brigadier

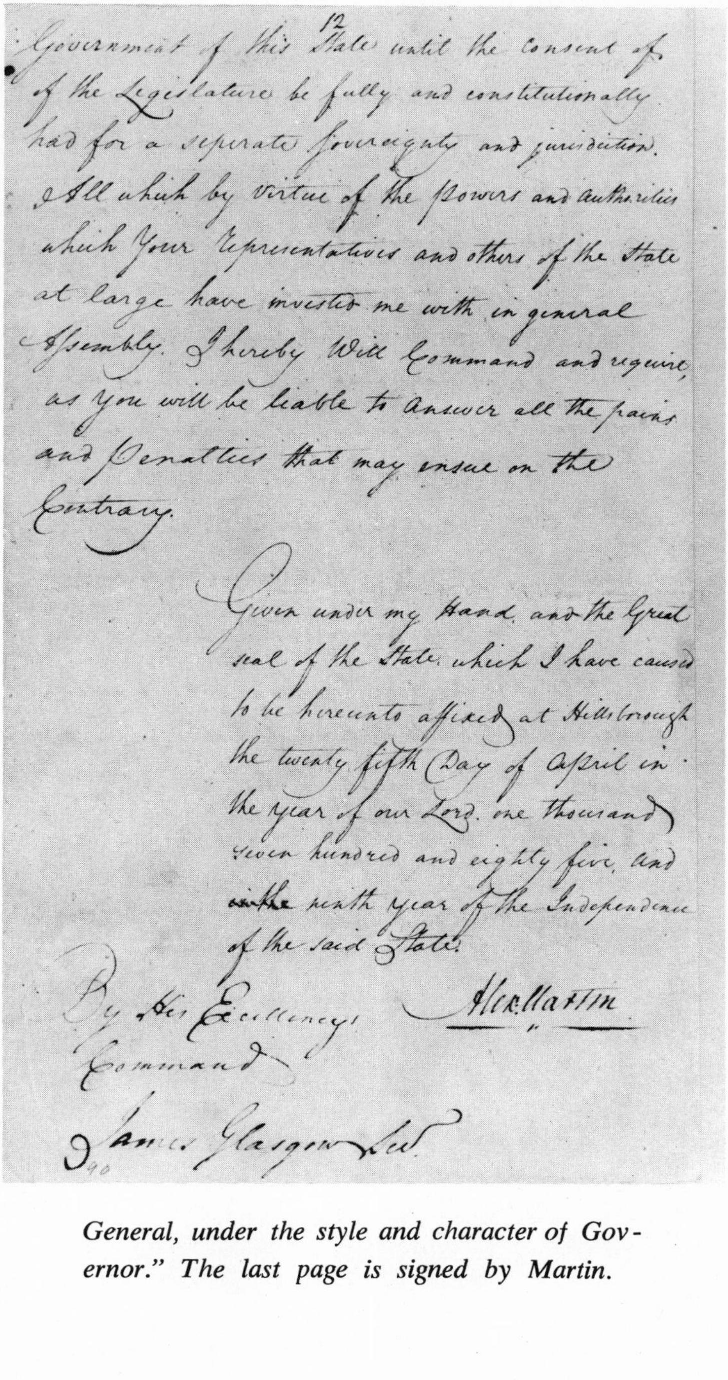

Government of this State until the consent of of the Legislature be fully and constitutionally had for a seperate Sovereignty and jurisdiction. All which by virtue of the Powers and authorities which Your Representatives and others of the State at large have invested me with in general Assembly. I hereby Will Command and require, as you will be liable to Answer all the pains and Penalties that may ensue on the Contrary.

Given under my Hand, and the Great seal of the State, which I have caused to be hereunto affixed at Hillsborough the twenty fifth Day of April in the year of our Lord, one thousand seven hundred and eighty five, and in the ninth year of the Independence of the said State

By His Excellency's
Command

Alex Martin

James Glasgow Sec.

General, under the style and character of Governor." The last page is signed by Martin.

Carolina's chief executive on May 1st. Richard Caswell, his successor, was a personal friend of many Franklinites, whom he had come to know when he had spent a year in the Cumberland. Caswell was more sympathetic to the ambitions of the frontiersmen, and they thought it unlikely that he would permit his legislature, no matter how angry its members might be, to order an invasion.

But John Sevier was not the type of man who could allow the Martin manifesto to go unchallenged. He received the official copy of the North Carolina document on May 8, 1785, and forty-eight hours later he answered it with an even firmer statement of his own. He was not one to waste words and said all that he felt necessary in four brief, pungent paragraphs:

STATE OF FRANKLIN
A Proclamation to the People

Whereas a manifesto is sent in and circulating this State, in order to create sedition and stir up insurrection among the good citizens of this State, thinking thereby to destroy that peace and tranquility that so greatly abounds among the peaceful citizens of the new, happy country.

And, not withstanding that their own acts declare to the world that they first invited us to the separation, if in their power, would now bring down ruin and destruction on that part of their late citizens, that the world well knows saved their State out of the hands of the enemy, and saved her from impending ruin.

Notwithstanding we have the fullest confidence in the true attitude of the good citizens of this State, particularly their attachment and fidelity to it, I have thought it proper to issue this Proclamation, strictly enjoining and requiring every and all good citizens of this State, as they will answer the same at peril, to be obedient and comfortable to the laws thereof.

Witness, John Sevier, Esq., Governor and Captain-General in and over the said State, under his hand and seal of arms, in Washington County, this tenth day of May, one thousand seven hundred and eighty five, and in the first year of our Independence.

JOHN SEVIER
GOD SAVE OUR STATE!

Anyone who had been thinking in terms of compromise now knew better. Franklin was willing to fight with either words or bullets, as her opponents desired. But, in one way or another, she was determined to preserve her freedom.

 *Chapter 4.*

SETTLING ACCOUNTS

NORTH CAROLINIANS AND OTHERS who opposed the independence of Franklin found it convenient in the spring and summer of 1785 to picture John Sevier as a bully who believed in settling all disputes with firearms—an impatient, unthinking man who used force to resolve every problem. They painted their propaganda portrait so effectively that this image of him has persisted down to the present day, almost two hundred years later. But they did him a grave injustice.

Sevier's record indicates that he was an exceptionally able diplomat who successfully used charm, tact and logic in preference to saber-rattling and who won his major victories with words rather than weapons. Twenty-four hours before he issued his proclamation defying North Carolina he wrote a long, friendly letter to Governor Richard Caswell of North Carolina. In it he outlined the new state's position, acknowledged Franklin's debt to the parent state and offered to settle all disputes over money, land and other issues amicably, in "the spirit of American brotherhood."

Caswell replied in the same vein, stressing that he could not imagine a situation in which wartime comrades-in-arms could take up arms against one another. He declared he was not in a position to say precisely what stand North Carolina would take, since her position would depend on the mood of the legislature, but he made it plain that he bore the men of the Cumberland no ill will.

This private correspondence made it unlikely that there would be a tragic clash between the militia of the two states. Therefore Sevier's proclamation, seen in its true perspective, must be recognized for what it really was: an attempt to bolster the morale of the people of Franklin.

Two weeks later he gave even more effective proof of his statesmanship. Accompanied by other members of the commission authorized to deal with the Indians, he met the chiefs of the Cherokee at the farm home of Major Samuel Henry, one of his principal militia officers. Sevier's opponents maligned him when they said he would rather fight savages than eat or sleep, for, like many frontiersmen, he felt great sympathy and understanding for the Indians.

The overall story of the relationship between the American settler and the native he displaced is one of the most shameful in the saga of the development and growth of the United States. The Indian was harassed and cheated and bullied, driven from his home and hunting grounds by strangers who outnumbered him, used more powerful weapons than he possessed and repeatedly broke solemn promises to him. It is small wonder that he fought to defend himself and his land and that he frequently resorted to brutality.

Sevier drove a hard bargain, acquiring for Franklin more territory than the frontiersmen had occupied under the terms of the treaty the Cherokee had signed with North Carolina. At the same time, he dealt honestly and honor-

ably with them, guaranteeing that he would respect their boundaries and would take every possible measure to make certain that the citizens of the new state did not encroach on Cherokee territory.

The chief executive of Franklin proved himself an able administrator in the state's domestic affairs, too. He supervised the appraisal of property by the officials of his Treasury and insisted that new settlers be allowed a period

Sevier granted new land-owners a two-year grace period before paying taxes, a policy carried on afterward as the American West was settled.

of two years to clear their land, plant crops and begin to earn a profit before starting to pay taxes. North Carolina had levied taxes on every landowner, including those who had just established homesteads beyond the mountains, and this principle had been a major cause of hostility on the part of the wilderness dwellers toward the mother state. Sevier made sure he did not repeat North Carolina's mistakes.

Eventually the two-year waiting period, or moratorium, was passed into law by the Franklin legislature. This liberal, far-seeing attitude was preserved to the end of Franklin's days, and, when it was incorporated into the new state of Tennessee more than a decade later, the Tennessee legislature passed a law that was identical. Countless thousands of pioneers who made their homes in the American West benefited from John Sevier's foresight, as other states later copied the laws on taxation that he was the first to sponsor.

It was obvious to the people of Franklin, if not to other parts of the country, that the new, self-proclaimed state was functioning efficiently and smoothly. It was William Cocke's task to persuade the Confederation Congress that Franklin was worthy of admission to the Union, and he arrived in New York, where Congress was meeting, in mid-May.

The petition, written by Cocke himself, was a clever document. It asked Congress to accept the cession of the Cumberland territory made to the United States by North Carolina and, simultaneously, to admit the new state of Franklin to membership in the Confederation. No mention

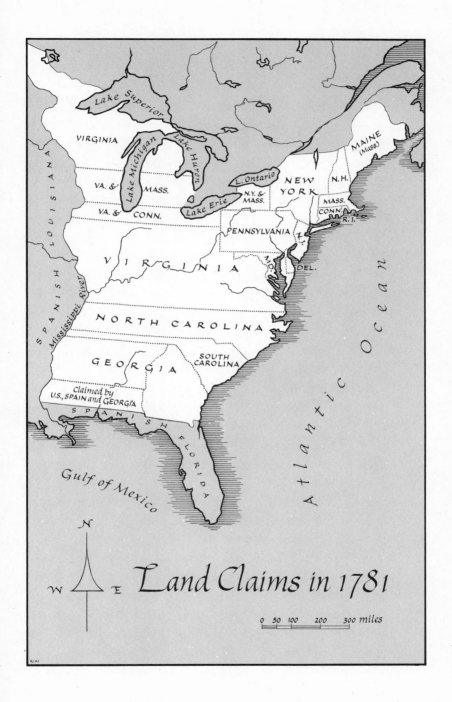

Land Claims in 1781

was made of the North Carolina act rescinding the cession of the territory.

The delegates from North Carolina promptly called the attention of Congress to this omission, of course, and Cocke was allowed to reply. He made an adroit speech, citing English common law, on which American law was based, and argued that the cession of the Cumberland, having been made, could not be repealed. "Can freedom be granted to a people with one hand, only to be taken away with the other?" he demanded. "This is not freedom, gentlemen. It is not the liberty for which you and I fought!"

A committee of members was appointed to study the question and reported back to Congress within a few days. To the delight of Cocke and the dismay of the North Carolinians, it was the unanimous opinion of the committee that, North Carolina having ceded her western territory to the United States, no subsequent act or law could repeal or nullify the cession.

The North Carolinians chose not to continue the argument and requested an immediate vote on a resolution accepting the cession of the Cumberland to the United States. Cocke immediately understood this seemingly contradictory stand.

Under the Articles of Confederation, two-thirds of the states were required to concur in a vote, on any subject, before it became the law of the United States. This "two-thirds rule" was already proving a handicap to the American government and was hampering its operations so badly that, two years later, virtually all of the states were demanding a stronger central government. It was this demand that was in part responsible for the Constitutional Convention of 1787 and the adoption of the new Constitution in 1789.

Cocke's friends from New England, the central Atlantic states and Georgia advised him they could not muster the necessary nine votes. All of the Southern states claimed territory in the West, and all but Georgia, which was young and struggling, were trying to protect their own interests. Cocke tried to delay the vote so he could work for additional support.

Only two states, Massachusetts and Delaware, favored such a delay. Both felt that the legal questions involved were so great that no vote should be taken until all aspects had been carefully considered. Both were openly sympathetic to the cause of Franklin, but, ironically, it was their lack of support that prevented Franklin from winning.

North Carolina, with nothing to lose in an immediate test, demanded that a vote be taken at once. Her delegates also announced that, since their state was a principal in the dispute, they would not cast a ballot. This seemingly noble stand was taken to impress the other states, but it fooled no one; the battle had been won.

The Confederation Congress voted on the question in a tense session on June 1, 1785. Those in favor were Connecticut, Rhode Island, New Hampshire, New York, Pennsylvania, New Jersey and Georgia. Maryland and Virginia were opposed, and the South Carolina delegation split its vote, thus putting the state, for all practical purposes, in the opposition. As Cocke feared, Massachusetts and Delaware abstained "with regret."

It was useless for Cocke to press a formal request that a vote be taken on Franklin's admission to the Union as a state, since the Articles of Confederation specified that the approval of nine states was necessary to win admission for any territory.

Since a majority of states had favored the cause of Franklin, Cocke had at least won a moral victory, and one of the North Carolina delegates wrote to Governor Caswell, complaining that the other states had demonstrated "a great degree of indelicacy and discourtesy."

The friends of Franklin were pleased, and Thomas Jefferson, who followed developments closely from Paris, where he was serving as United States Minister to France, predicted that both Franklin and Kentucky soon would be admitted to the Union. A strong champion of the West, he believed that his own Virginia and North Carolina were wrong to oppose what he believed to be the natural progress of the country.

Men in Franklin were so pleased to have won Jefferson's support that a movement was started to rename the state for him, but Sevier, Cocke and the other responsible leaders quickly stifled the attempt. No matter how great Jefferson's support, they would not allow their people to honor Jefferson at Benjamin Franklin's expense.

The Franklin controversy aroused interest in England. A number of newspapers there taunted the United States by pointing out that Americans had fought for their liberty because they had been taxed without representation in the British government, but now the free and independent United States was denying this same right to some of her own citizens.

Americans were embarrassed, and some of the most influential citizens sympathized with the self-proclaimed state of Franklin. General George Washington believed her cause right, but felt it would be improper for him to make a public statement on the issue, since he held no office. The correspondence of James Madison subsequently revealed that he felt as Washington did.

It is unlikely that William Cocke knew Franklin had the support of future United States Presidents, but he nevertheless felt encouraged when he returned home from New York. Enough states had upheld Franklin to convince him that admission to the Union would be won in time.

New tactics were needed, however, and he plunged into a series of conferences with Governor Sevier and other leaders. North Carolina was the stumbling block preventing Franklin's admission to the Union, so it seemed obvious that every effort should be made to win her approval.

The Assembly was called into session and convened at Jonesboro on August 1, 1785. A series of resolutions calculated to appease North Carolina were passed after brief debate. One provided that Franklin could collect any money owed by one of her citizens to the state of North Carolina and that these funds would be sent promptly to the North Carolina authorities. Another provided that funds belonging to North Carolina at the time of the separation, which happened to have been stored in Jonesboro and Greeneville, be repaid to the government of North Carolina immediately. This was a gesture, not a significant act; the sums were very small, amounting to less than three hundred dollars.

The most significant of the measures to come before the Franklin Assembly read, "Be it resolved that a commissioner be appointed to wait upon the General Assembly

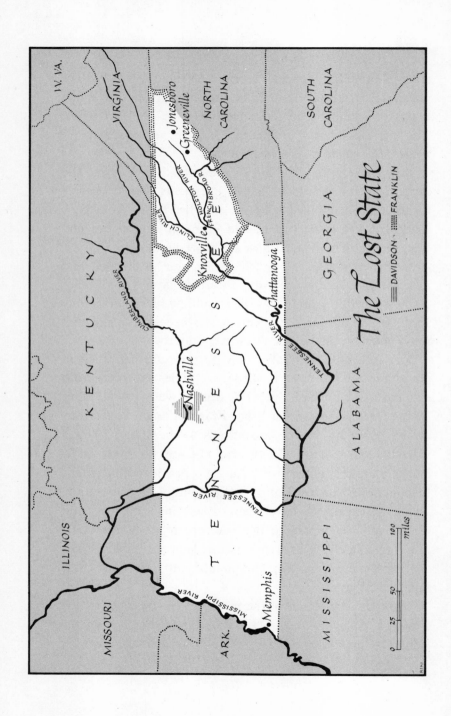

The Lost State

||||| DAVIDSON   ::::: FRANKLIN

of the State of North Carolina in order to convince them that it is our desire to establish a lasting and permanent union as well with North Carolina as the rest of the States on the continent; and to remove any doubts that may arise in that State respecting the goodness of our wishes towards them on the subject of our separation, and to assure them that we are determined to pay the most strict observance to the true intent and meaning of the act of cession passed in June, 1784."

The resolution passed the legislature by unanimous vote, Sevier and Cocke having explained their conciliatory tactics to every member. Even those who felt that North Carolina had become the "enemy" were persuaded to vote for the measure.

The necessary signatures were affixed to it in both chambers of the legislature the moment it was passed, and the ink had not yet dried when a sergeant-at-arms carried the document to Governor Sevier. He signed it at once, making it law, and then hurried off to the small, three-room log cabin that served as his own office.

There he wrote a letter to Governor Caswell, informing him of the measure, saying that a commissioner would be sent and asking if Caswell approved of the man he had in mind. This gesture was itself not only courteous but remarkably conciliatory.

Sevier showed great wisdom in his contemplated appointment. The man he chose for the difficult task was Thomas Stewart, a member of the Franklin Assembly who had long been prominent in the North Carolina legislature, before moving to a new home across the mountains. Although dedicated to the establishment of the infant state and determined to help win its recognition, Stewart had maintained a great many close friendships with the men in the parent state who had been his colleagues. He appeared to be an ideal selection for the post.

Governor Caswell was delighted and accepted the appointment. So, late in the autumn, Stewart went to North Carolina and made it his business to visit a number of prominent legislators before they convened in formal session. He also held several meetings with Caswell, who continued to express his sympathy for Franklin.

On December 21, 1785, the North Carolina legislature met, and on the same day Governor Caswell sent to it the Franklin resolutions along with a message saying that Stewart was on hand, eager for the opportunity to appear in person before the assemblage to explain the acts of the Franklin Assembly and win the friendship of the mother state.

The North Carolinians' initial response was encouraging. A bill was passed granting pardons to all citizens of the "rebel counties" who had worked for the establishment of Franklin, accepted offices in her executive or legislative branches or enlisted in her militia. Stewart sent an enthusiastic letter to Governor Sevier, predicting that the reconciliation soon would be complete.

However, he completely misjudged the temper of the North Carolina legislature. Another act was passed, stating that undoubtedy there were men in the West who were loyal to the parent state and wanted representation in her legislature. The bill provided the machinery that would—in theory—enable them to vote for such representatives.

This measure was intended as a first step toward readmitting the territory to the jurisdiction of North Carolina. It showed no understanding of the temperament and character of the frontiersmen. It was insulting, patronizing and, by rebuffing an extended hand of friendship, was certain to cause ill will. Not satisfied with this rejection, the North Carolina legislature made certain that the wedge separating the state from her offspring was driven even deeper.

No official recognition was taken of the Franklin resolutions, and the opponents of Franklin saw to it that neither chamber even heard readings of the documents. Finally, in the rudest of slights, no attention was paid to Stewart, who waited in vain for an invitation to address his former colleagues. Many of them dined with him, but made it plain they were keeping up a relationship with him only on a personal basis.

Stewart went home, fuming, and Franklin reacted vehemently. Even the moderates who might have been willing to resume North Carolina citizenship under terms guaranteeing improved representation in the legislature and greater financial aid for the new communities of the West were outraged. William Cocke summed up the reaction of the Franklinites in a letter to a young politician, saying, "North Carolina has lost all of her friends here. It is only with the greatest of effort that our Assembly has been prevented from passing a vindictive bill putting a price on the heads of all who voted against us."

Thrown back on their own resources and thoroughly disillusioned, the wilderness men decided to adopt a new technique, one that required both self-control and statesmanship. Rather than become embroiled in a feud that could only hurt both sides, they made up their minds to ignore North Carolina. From that time forward they would act as though the parent state did not exist.

First, however, they wanted to prove they were strong and growing stronger. The Assembly, still convening at Jonesboro, passed a bill establishing a new county, Blount, in territory to the south of the older counties. A few short years earlier this region had been uninhabited wilderness, and the creation of a new county was intended to prove that Franklin was expanding rapidly.

This move, as it happened, was premature. The judiciary had not yet moved into Blount County, and law enforcement agencies, tax collection offices and even surveying units had not been appointed to serve there. Another six months would pass before the new county was able to function.

In any event, there were eight counties in the state now, and the legislature issued a directive for a new convention to be held in a few months. Its purpose would be to make the temporary constitution permanent or to amend it in such ways as the voters might see fit. "We're going forward," Judge Campbell wrote, "no matter how hard our foes might try to prevent our growth. In one way and another, we shall maintain the independence we have won."

Perhaps the most encouraging sign of prosperity to the Franklinites was the ever-increasing tide of immigration. Neither the opposition of North Carolina nor the inability of the Confederation Congress to recognize the new state halted the newcomers, who continued to cross the mountains in ever-increasing numbers. In fact, Franklin's troubles seemed to encourage "men of independent spirits to cast their lot with us," as Sevier declared in a New Year's Day proclamation.

The immigrants came not only from North Carolina, but from many of the larger cities, too. New York, which had been occupied by the British during the better part of the war, was finding it difficult to reestablish a prospering economy. Unemployment was widespread, and her poor, many of Scottish extraction, moved to Franklin.

Immigrants from the British Isles also were settling in Franklin. Men from England, Scotland and Ireland who had not been able to leave the Old World during the war were crossing the Atlantic again, and the uproar created in the English press over Franklin's problems persuaded the most rugged of them that they should make their homes in the new state, where liberty was prized above all else.

Consequently the caliber of Franklin's newcomers was high, and these men, often accompanied by their wives and children, were already prepared to face hardships, lacks of convenience and even personal danger. They adapted themselves to their new environment quickly and easily, the majority making the transition so smoothly that Colonel Campbell wrote, "It is almost impossibe to distinguish between our new citizens and the old, so readily have our immigrants become one with us."

No precise figures are available, but it has been estimated that at least five thousand families settled in Franklin during the last six months of 1785 and that an additional five thousand or more arrived during the first half of 1786. These estimates may be too low. It is known that approx-

Franklin's newcomers—with their wives and children—were prepared to face hardship and danger.

imately one thousand families went to Nashville in the autumn of 1785, and it is believed that far more established homesteads in the older portions of the territory. This makes sense, since Nashville was the real frontier, where personal dangers were greater. It was far more convenient for immigrants to claim fertile land for themselves in areas easier to reach, as it was still necessary to

cross dense forests in order to make a journey as far as Nashville.

Franklinites boasted that they were citizens of the fastest-developing state in the Union, and the claim may have been valid. A rural, one-room school about twenty-five miles from Jonesboro that was occupied by only three boys in September, 1785, was overflowing by thirty-two pupils the following spring. Knoxville, which was founded early in 1786 by a settler from North Carolina named James White and was first known as White's Fort, had a population of more than two thousand by the end of the same year. A mill in New London, Connecticut, that made wool increased the number of bolts it sent to the Cumberland by more than six hundred percent between the summer of 1785 and 1786.

Skillets, pots and other cooking utensils, all of them made in the older parts of the country, were so expensive that an iron foundry was established near Greeneville in November, 1787. At first it specialized in making nails. The handling of mail was a state-administered function, and in late 1785 there was five postmasters on the Franklin payroll. A scant year later the number had increased to one hundred and twenty-six.

The boom dazed even the most optimistic of the early pioneers, who found their most extravagant predictions coming true. A man could clear a homestead in the recesses of a vast forest, many miles from his nearest neighbor and within a few months find that the entire forest had vanished. Prices of fertile valley property rose so sharply and rapidly that land speculation became a mania, and everyone who had reserves of capital to spare, even a few dollars, invested every penny. Governor Sevier, Justice Campbell and the other high-ranking officials of Franklin bought and sold land with almost reckless abandon, and so did the newest immigrants from the slums of London or the poverty-stricken hills of Scotland. Those who had no funds, borrowed them, and bankers who charged exorbitant interest rates enjoyed higher profits than anyone else.

As choice farmlands disappeared, it was tragically inevitable that new arrivals searching for homesteads should spill out beyond the borders of Franklin into the preserves of the Cherokee. Ordinarily the leaders of the tribes would have protested immediately, and it might have been possible for the authorities of Franklin to slow the tide, if not halt it. But the Indians themselves were going through a period of major change.

The Cherokee, contrary to the belief of settlers who knew no better, were not a single, united people but a loosely knit family of tribes. They had been held together for years by a wise and powerful chief, Oconostota, called the "Great Warrior" by all of the Cherokee.

In the summer of 1785, just at the period when immigration into Franklin was reaching a peak and the newcomers began encroaching on Indian territory, Oconostota died. The months that followed were bewildering to his followers, and, with no one leader to direct their destinies, the subtribes of the nation were incapable of working together.

So, in helpless rage, they watched the settlers occupying their hunting grounds, and by the spring of 1786 some of the best portions of the forest, where game abounded, had been cleared away by the axes of the immigrants. As every Cherokee warrior well knew, this seizure of land broke both the letter and the spirit of the solemn treaty that Governor Sevier had signed with the elders of their nation.

It was natural that the Indians wanted to drive out the foreigners who were illegally and wantonly destroying the wilderness on which the Cherokee depended for their food, clothing and shelter. It was natural, too, that braves who were forced to make the cruel choice of seeing their families starve or beat a cowardly retreat farther into the forest should yearn for revenge against men they considered cruel and ruthless thieves.

By the time Governor Sevier and other Franklin authorities learned the extent of the encroachment, it was too late to turn back the waves of immigrants. An explosive situation had been created, and the frontiersmen who knew and understood the Indians realized that a vicious frontier war might break out at any time.

Chapter 5.

THE "GOLDEN ERA"

WHILE THE CHEROKEE secretly prepared for war, the citizens of Franklin were busy clearing land, farming, building and making plans for their new constitutional convention. The demand for new schools was insatiable, and within a few years a number of institutions of higher learning were founded, among them Greeneville College in Greene County, Cumberland College in Nashville and Blount College in Knoxville. One of the most impressive features of life in expanding Franklin was the constant yearning of her people for more and better schools.

Churches followed the new immigrants, too, and by 1786 the larger communities no longer relied on circuit-riding ministers but supported their own, permanent clergymen. Since so many immigrants were either Scots or of Scottish descent, it was natural that most churches should be Presbyterian, the principal faith of Scotland.

The clergy exerted a strong civilizing influence on Franklin, and the coarseness of the Cumberland's early days rapidly dissipated. Ministers delivered thundering sermons condemning profanity and overindulgence in alcohol, public brawling and gambling, and the state's leaders were urged to set an example of sober respectability. The influx of women and children also helped to tame the raucous frontier spirits of the wilderness men, and, when John Sevier appeared in church dressed in a conservative black suit with white silk stockings and buckled shoes, a white shirt and a linen stock, his friends scarcely recognized him. A new era had been inaugurated.

In 1784 there were no public houses in Franklin with accomodations for travelers, who either found private families with whom to stay or slept in the open. But merchants began to visit the state in large numbers, as did horse dealers and other men of business. Lawyers were required to follow the courts from one town to another, and physicians, frantically busy because of the need for their services, were always on the move. Therefore, by 1786, inns dotted the entire state. There were several in Jonesboro, some of them built for the exclusive use of legislators and state officials, and at least two had opened their doors in Greeneville. Plans were being made to erect a handsome brick hostelry in Nashville, and a few years later the Nashville Inn became renowned throughout the West.

Meals served at the inns were simple, with an emphasis placed on plain cooking and hearty portions. Cooks were required to put forth their best efforts at all times; a guest who was served a burned dish or spoiled meat might stalk into the kitchen, pistol in hand, to demand retribution. The raw spirit of the wilderness was not completely gone.

The inns became gathering places for the men of every community, and no woman ever thought of appearing in one. A private home, usually a log cabin but occasionally a clapboard house, was the place for wives and daughters. Only the men gathered at the inns to share a meal or a drink, gossip and exchange news, political matters being a primary topic of conversation.

The permanent constitution was discussed in detail, and gradually the basic demands of the voters emerged and became clarified. By the time the delegates elected to the convention buckled down to business in Greeneville early in 1786, the opinions of the citizens were almost universally recognized. As a result there was little discussion of most issues—but not all.

Franklinites, like all Americans, wanted a sharp division in the powers of state and church, so a clause in the permanent constitution specified that no minister of the gospel could hold a seat in the state legislature or accept public office. At the same time, however, every citizen was guaranteed full religious liberty and the right to worship as he pleased.

Care was taken, too, to insure that no one man or group become too powerful. The voters wanted to keep a tight rein on those who ruled in their name, so it was agreed that the Governor would be elected annually, as would the legislature. No appointed official could hold office beyond the tenure of the Governor who had appointed him.

An unexpected storm was caused by the provision excluding clergymen from office, and Cocke, who was the presiding officer, had his hands full. The Reverend Houston took exception to the measure, and so did the Reverend Hezekiah Balch. Houston was a delegate to the convention, but it is not clear whether Balch also had been elected or whether he was a visitor who was granted the privilege of taking part in the debate. In any event, the two ministers launched a furious attack on the provision, and some of the more devout delegates supported them.

Their stand drove the advocates of the separation of state and church powers into a frenzy, and the debate became violent. Men exchanged personal insults on the floor of the convention, challenged each other to duels and on two or three occasions had fist fights. Neither Cocke nor Sevier, in spite of their strength, their wisdom or their experience in dealing with warring Indians, could halt the feud.

Houston acidly reminded the convention that it was meeting in Greeneville's First Presbyterian Church, and Balch added that if the building did not contaminate the members, surely a clergyman could not harm his fellow citizens by holding a public office.

Their foes countered by moving that the convention move to Greeneville's largest tavern and hold its sessions there.

The Reverend Balch thundered that he would not attend a meeting "in a house of debauchery, where men may swill whisky and ale until they lose their wits." The supporters of the ministers threatened to walk out of the convention if the site was changed.

The controversy spread beyond the confines of the meeting, and citizens throughout the state took sides. Someone, possibly a delegate to the convention, wrote and printed a handbill, presenting a long list of reasons why clergymen should be excluded from office.

The ministers retaliated, through friends in the judiciary, to halt the distribution of the handbill. In Washington County a judge of the circuit court declared that the document contained "treasonable insinuations against the United States, and false and ungenerous reflections against persons of distinction in the ecclesiastical department, fraught with falsehood, calculated to alienate the minds of their citizens from their government and overturn the same.

"Upon mature deliberation, the court condemned said handbill to be publicly burned by the High Sheriff as a treasonable, wicked, false and seditious libel."

The quarrel became so intense and bitter that both sides finally realized that, if allowed to continue, it could divide the Franklinites into two permanently opposed factions. If this happened, the very existence of the state would be jeopardized.

The debate became calmer, and, when the issue was put to a vote, the advocates of the separation of church and state won an easy victory. The provision barring office to clergymen was incorporated into the permanent constitution. The ministers and their friends did not let the question die, and the Reverend Houston published a pamphlet on the subject. But the bitter heat had dissipated from the controversy.

In the main, the people were satisfied with their new constitution. Their liberties were guaranteed, they were assured that a working government could operate efficiently, and they had every reasonable safeguard incorporated into the constitution to prevent office-holders from gaining too much power.

The year 1786 was the "golden era" in Franklin's brief history. Settlers by the thousands continued to arrive, most of them settling near the Tennessee, Nolichucky and Holston Rivers. No one went hungry, the government was functioning with surprising smoothness, and, most important, the state was at peace.

For the moment, North Carolina was content not to press her claim for the restoration of her territory. Governor Caswell took no action because of his sympathy for the aims of the West, and the legislature refrained from taking the initiative, because its members realized that the Confederation Congress, the only place the claim could be settled in her favor, was disposed to take the side of the Cumberlanders.

The Cherokee seemed content, although surface appearances were deceptive. Their plans to launch a war of retaliation were abandoned—at least temporarily. The Confederation Congress signed two treaties with the Indians in 1786, marking the first time the national government had stepped in to represent all the states. The Cherokee assumed that the government of all Americans was more powerful than that of an individual state and therefore believed the agreement would be honored. They were not aware of two important factors. Congress was weak, unable to impose its will on any state that chose not to honor its treaties. And Franklin, which had not been recognized as a state, had no delegates in Congress. So the wilderness men saw no reason why they should accept treaties in which they had been given no voice.

Immigrants were continuing to push into the preserves of the Cherokee, who felt doubly cheated, of course, which made their righteous anger all the greater. But the day of retribution had not yet arrived.

In the late spring of 1786 the Franklin Assembly held another session in Jonesboro, and so little is known of its deliberations that the names of its presiding officers were not recorded for posterity. Apparently it concerned itself with routine matters.

One bill passed during that session, however, was significant. The legislators felt the state was secure enough to give Colonel Charles Robertson the power to establish a mint and coin thirty thousand dollars in Franklin currency. Robertson found someone with artistic ability to design the coins, in denominations of one dollar, fifty cents and twenty-five cents, and the presses were made for him at a Greeneville iron foundry.

Robertson promised the legislature the coins would be made within three weeks, and letters of thanks addressed to him by Treasury officials indicate he kept his word. According to descriptions of the period, all of the coins bore a reproduction of the state seal on one side; on the other, the dollar carried an engraving of mountains, the half-dollar showed a poplar tree, and the quarter a pair of crossed, long rifles. Nothing is known of the sizes of the coins, or of the metals used in making them. Since gold was scarce, it is likely they were of silver, perhaps mixed with lead and brass.

It is virtually impossible to find Franklin coins today,

and no pictures or drawings of them exist anywhere. They vanished soon after Franklin itself disappeared. Most of them were probably melted down, and perhaps a few found their way into the souvenir hoards of individuals. It has been said that collectors would pay a fortune for a genuine Franklin coin.

The attempt to gain recognition as a state continued in 1786. William Cocke was reappointed as the representative of Franklin to the Continental Congress, but the atmosphere in New York had not changed, so Cocke did not bother to make another journey there. Instead he sought the advice of Benjamin Franklin, to whom he wrote a long letter in mid-June.

The most revered of living Americans replied two months later. The state was wise, he said, not to continue its dispute with North Carolina, and he doubted that direct negotiations could solve the problem. The best method of obtaining recognition, he believed, would be through the good offices of the Confederation Congress, "a wise and impartial tribunal, which can have no sinister views to warp its judgment." He also showed his awareness of the opposition to recognition on the part of Virginia, South Carolina and other states by counseling patience and cultivating friendships.

Franklin's leaders carefully followed his suggestions and took particular pains to attain a closer relationship with Georgia. The least developed of the original Thirteen States, Georgia was remarkably similar to Franklin in many ways. She had no large cities and few industries, most of her citizens earned their living as farmers, and frontier conditions prevailed in the better part of her territory.

There was no need for William Cocke to remind his colleagues that Georgia had been the only state in the South that had been an enthusiastic supporter of Franklin's bid for statehood before the Confederation Congress. And the attitude of Georgians expressed itself in other ways, too. Visitors from Franklin were given a warm welcome everywhere in Georgia, while North Carolinians were made to feel uncomfortable there.

Governor Sevier sent a letter to Governor Edward Telfair of Georgia, proposing the appointment of a joint commission to establish a mutually satisfactory border. Telfair replied promptly and cordially, agreeing to the idea. Both states sent representatives familiar with the area, and by mid-summer a border line was drawn. Within a few weeks the legislatures of both states ratified the agreement, and Colonel Campbell wrote to his brother, "Georgia treats us in a manner we deserve, as an equal."

In August, 1786, Governor Telfair approached Franklin with a scheme. The Creek Indians were on the warpath in Georgia's territorial lands, later to become Alabama, and he suggested a joint military campaign to quiet the uprising.

Franklin was eager to cooperate, but had to postpone a decision. Sevier had seen signs that the Cherokee were stirring and wanted to learn more about their intentions before he dissipated his strength by sending a corps to Georgia. Aware of the need for haste, he assured Telfair he would act quickly and immediately dispatched several hunters and scouts into Cherokee country, which extended to the Mississippi River.

An unexpected political situation further hampered the Franklin authorities. The North Carolina legislature passed a bill setting a date for an "election" in the territory it still claimed, and under the terms of this measure the citizens would indicate whether or not they wanted to return to the authority of the mother state.

Sevier was annoyed and swore he would not permit another state to set up polling places on the sovereign soil of Franklin. But others, perhaps Cocke and Judge Campbell, persuaded him that there was a far better way to foil North Carolina's intentions. The scheme the Franklin authorities evolved was a rather complicated one, and no records were kept to indicate its author or authors. Since the Franklin judiciary was deeply involved, the credit probably belongs to the Chief Justice.

Polling places were set up, and the purpose of the balloting was widely advertised. In each district the Circuit Court judge for that area was in charge, assisted by his bailiffs and sheriffs. Franklin refused to compromise its standing by permitting outsiders to take charge and insisted on conducting the voting itself. But members of the North Carolina legislature, judiciary and "such other persons as may be deemed competent by the Governor of North Carolina" were invited to all polling places as observers, and an official proclamation signed by Governor Sevier promised that the North Carolinians could be present to watch closely when the individual ballots were counted.

Unfortunately, the total figure for all of Franklin has not been preserved. Perhaps the records were lost in the years between the time Franklin vanished and reappeared as part of Tennessee. Or it may be that Sevier and his associates were so contemptuous of North Carolina that they made no attempt to keep a permanent tally.

Sevier was annoyed and swore he would not permit North Carolina to set up polling places in Franklin.

There were as yet no newspapers in the West, and, when the results of the balloting became known, no self-respecting North Carolina newspaper would print them. The general tenor of the voting was clear and is indicated in the correspondence, official and personal, of both Franklinites and North Carolinians.

Franklin won a resounding victory. At literally every polling place an overwhelming majority of voters rejected reunion with North Carolina. A few of the figures that were kept for posterity indicate the extent of the sweep. For example, two hundred and fifty-four citizens went to the polls at what was called "the main election station" in Jonesboro. Of these, two hundred and thirty-nine voted against a return of the Cumberland to North Carolina. At a place called Rennoe's, on Sinking Creek in Washington County, one hundred and seventy-nine ballots were cast. All but five rejected North Carolinian sovereignty.

In their subsequent correspondence the observers from North Carolina were forced to concede that the polling had been scrupulously honest and that no returns had been altered. But the North Carolina legislature could not tolerate such a stinging defeat and issued a bristling statement, charging that the Franklinites had intimidated voters, who had been afraid to express their true sentiments.

This claim was hotly denied by Franklin, and it is likely that the balloting was a true, fair test. At no time in Franklin's history was there a movement favoring a return to the jurisdiction of North Carolina, and very few men ever indicated such feelings.

While the political battle was still raging, Sevier continued to correspond with Governor Telfair of Georgia on the prospect of launching a joint expedition against the Creek, and the latter sent the adjutant-general of his militia, Major George Elholm, to visit Franklin and coordinate plans. Major Elholm was a remarkable man and was destined to play a major role in the military development of the infant state.

European by birth, Elholm came from the Duchy of Holstein, which at that time was part of the kingdom of Denmark. Like so many of his neighbors, he spoke German rather than Danish, and, finding opportunities for advancement rather limited, he became a soldier of fortune, serving as a mercenary in the armies of several German principalities. He held the rank of Captain at the time the American Revolution broke out.

Attracted by the Americans' yearnings for independence and their high-principled concepts of personal liberties, he came to the New World early in the war and was one of a band of devoted foreigners who served in the Continental Army with loyalty and distinction. He was with a small group of taskmasters who transformed General George Washington's rabble into a disciplined, trained corps at Valley Forge. Later he served as a cavalry officer in the South and spent a number of months with the raiders of South Carolina's Brigadier General Francis Marion, who developed a type of guerrilla hit-and-run warfare that has been utilized down to the present day.

In the final months of the war Elholm was a member of the staff of General Anthony Wayne in Georgia and performed so brilliantly that the Georgia legislature gave him a tract of land and invited him to make his home there. He accepted, but was not interested in farming and became adjutant-general of the state's militia. There was little for him to do, however, and, having become increasingly bored, he was pleased to accept the mission that Governor Telfair gave him.

Three battalions of Franklin militia were mustered for his inspection, and Elholm was horrified by their lack of training and military discipline. All that could be said in their favor was that, like all frontiersmen, they were superb marksmen.

Unable to remain silent, he made his views known. Sevier and his officers were sensitive to criticism by outsiders and would have resented such interference from most non-Franklinites, but Elholm was different. He had proved himself in battle under Marion and Wayne, and some of the Franklin officers had served with him. Sevier and his high-ranking officers listened and were impressed.

As commander-in-chief of the militia, John Sevier was free to take any steps he found necessary to improve the condition of his army and promptly offered Elholm the adjutant-generalship of the Franklin forces. Elholm accepted on the condition that he would be given a free hand to train the troops as he saw fit. Sevier and the officers agreed, and Elholm resigned his Georgia commission, put his property there up for sale and accepted a tract of land near Jonesboro.

He went to work with enthusiastic vigor and first trained a cadre of officers, then one of sergeants to help him. His experience was infinitely greater than that of anyone else in Franklin, and he worked with a concentrated fury that was typical of everything he did. From the early autumn of 1786 until the disappearance of Franklin as a state, Elholm continued to train the militia, and it was almost exclusively because of his efforts that the regiments there became the finest in the West. When the state of Tennessee came into being a few years later, it was not accidental that her militia units were better organized and far better disciplined than those of virtually any other state. Elholm did his work well and created a fighting force capable of meeting any foe in either formal or frontier warfare.

There was one unfortunate result of his transfer of allegiance. Governor Telfair of Georgia was annoyed because his adjutant-general had been "stolen" and did not hesitate to make his feelings and those of his legislators known to the upstarts across the border. Sevier sent back an equally angry reply, and relations between Franklin and Georgia became so strained that plans for conducting a joint expedition against the Creek had to be postponed.

The Indians still threatened both states, however, and Telfair took matters into his own hands to prevent an uprising. Aware that the Creek had no idea of his unexpected feud with Franklin, he sent commissioners to deal with the tribe's chiefs and deliberately misled them by giving the impression that troops from both Georgia and Franklin would be sent against them unless they signed a new peace treaty.

The Creek had great respect for Major Elholm and, knowing he was now training the Franklin regiments, decided to come to terms before being subjected to intolerable punishment. They signed Telfair's treaty, and Franklin enjoyed the benefits of peace on her southern border, without having had to exert any efforts on her own behalf. It was small wonder that Sevier felt smugly pleased with himself.

Neither he nor anyone else in Franklin could relax and enjoy the benefits of statehood, however, until the disagreement with North Carolina was ended and the fledgling state was admitted to the Union. The Franklin legislature convened in Mid-November, 1786, and Governor Sevier appeared before a joint session to urge that another attempt be made to persuade North Carolina to accept the inevitable and give up her claims to the lands across the mountains.

The legislature promptly passed a bill urging that "a concerted effort be made to reconcile our differences with our former parent, North Carolina." William Cocke and Judge Campbell were elected as special commissioners to go to North Carolina for the purpose of establishing amicable relations.

The mission ran into difficulties from the outset. Judge Campbell fell ill and suffered from a high fever for ten days, at the end of which he was too weak to travel. Rather than resign his post, however, he wrote a long letter to Governor Caswell and the North Carolina legislature, exerting himself beyond his physical capacity and, as a direct result, losing his sight in one eye.

Cocke went to North Carolina alone, taking his colleague's letter with him, and sent a petition to the North Carolina legislature, asking to be heard in a joint session of both houses. It was virtually impossible for the North Carolinians to refuse his request. Not only had Cocke been a battlefield comrade of many of the legislators, but everyone knew of Judge Campbell's sacrifice. No elected official dared to risk the displeasure of voters who would be sure to resent a snub to a man whose patriotism had resulted in the loss of an eye.

So Cocke was granted formal permission to address a joint session of the legislature. His appearance on December 16, 1786, aroused sufficient interest to fill every seat on the floor and crowd the galleries.

Cocke made the most of his opportunity. First he read Judge Campbell's letter and then announced quietly that the effort had resulted in the loss of sight in one eye. Finally he launched into his own address and spoke for more than four hours. Never had his oratory been more impressive, and he presented urgent reasons for North Carolina's dismissal of her claims to her frontier territory.

Franklin, Cocke said, was an underpopulated land, in spite of her rapid growth. Her citizens lived under conditions that people in more advanced parts of the United States would consider primitive. To her west was the vast and powerful Cherokee nation, to the southwest were the Choctaw, and directly to the south were the Creek. If all of the Indians made war against Franklin simultaneously, the frontiersmen would be overwhelmed.

But, until the argument with North Carolina was settled, no funds could be made available by the Confederation Congress for the purpose of strengthening the militia and obtaining additional arms and gunpowder. The wilderness dwellers were being forced to rely only on themselves and their own slender resources. In the name of humanity, Cocke begged, the mother state should free her offspring.

Having made an appeal on emotional grounds, he presented a long legal brief, proving the right of Franklin to secede from North Carolina and set up her own government. His performance was superb, and his audience applauded him at length when, his voice hoarse and his clothes soaked with perspiration, he finally sat down.

Neither his address nor Judge Campbell's letter changed

the minds of the North Carolinians, however. Many felt great sympathy for their brothers in the wilderness, but they had no intention of giving up their claims to some of the most fertile land in the United States. The right of separation was flatly and unequivocally denied.

The attitude of North Carolina was so rigid that several observers from Nashville expressed great indignation at the treatment given the wilderness dwellers, and Cocke went home with one consolation easing his journey. Even though he had failed, it was possible that Nashville and the other settlements to the west of Franklin might throw in their lot with the new state.

Chapter 6

STATEHOOD, INDEPENDENCE— OR SURRENDER?

THE ATTEMPTS OF FRANKLIN to achieve independent statehood and gain admittance to the Union were not unique. In 1786 movements occurred simultaneously in newly developing American territories that were in many ways remarkably similar to the political upheavals that took place in Africa during the years immediately following World War II, when the colonies there that had long belonged to the major European powers declared their independence and established new nations.

Agitation for the separation of the Vermont District from New Hampshire became so intense during 1786 that responsible men in New Hampshire were willing to admit privately what they would not yet concede publicly: the inevitability of statehood for Vermont. The Maine District of Massachusetts was in ferment, too, and representatives of every Maine township met in Portland during the summer of 1786 to demand the right to set up a state of their own. Independence for Kentucky was virtually assured, although the citizens of that District believed that Virginia was subjecting them to delaying tactics.

Seen in retrospect, however, the attitude of Virginia was liberal. Late in 1785 Kentucky requested independent statehood, and in January, 1786, the Virginia legislature agreed, provided a convention was held in the District in September of that year; if it approved, statehood would be granted by June of 1787. The Virginia resolution also stipulated that the consent of Congress would be required.

Far-seeing Kentuckians realized their cause was won, but the majority of the District's citizens were impetuous and impatient and thought that Virginia was delaying in the hope that the independence movement would die out. There was talk in Kentucky as there was in neighboring Franklin, that the two Districts should unite and, if necessary, form an independent nation.

In order to understand the mood of the West in 1786 and 1787 it is essential that the differences between Eighteenth century patriotism and that of later periods be recognized. The independence of the United States from Great Britain had been won by a minority of the citizens of the thirteen former English colonies, and there were many who were made uncomfortable by the realization that they no longer owed fealty to the Crown.

Americans had no single tradition that united them as one people, and the loyalty of many was further weakened by the severe economic depression that struck the country in the years immediately following the war. Thousands who were unable to find employment and feed their families migrated to the West, and they, of all Americans, felt the least devotion to a new nation with a fumbling, weak Congress and inadequate national leadership.

In 1786, when the clamor for separation reached its peak in both Franklin and Kentucky, a new danger arose to complicate the situation. Businessmen in the East, anxious to expand their trade and find new markets, encouraged the Confederation Congress to negotiate with Spain, which was seeking a trade treaty with the infant nation.

John Jay was delegated to negotiate a trade treaty with Spain.

In July, 1786, Congress authorized Secretary of Foreign Affairs John Jay to open talks with the new Spanish envoy who had just arrived in New York for the purpose.

Soon the basic outlines of Spanish policy became clear. She was willing to grant extensive trade rights to the United States, on the condition that the new nation admit Spanish sovereignty over the Mississippi River. On only this one subject was Don Diego de Gardoqui, the Spanish minister, stubbornly adamant. He was willing to adjust the American-Spanish colonial border in a way that would grant additional territory to the United States, and the trade terms he offered were exceptionally generous. But he insisted that the United States admit the Mississippi was a Spanish river and that Spain had the right to close the stream to American shipping for as long as twenty-five to thirty years, if she chose to exercise this power.

The Mississippi was vital to the settlers in Franklin, Kentucky and other parts of the West. The growers of tobacco, cotton and food products had discovered they could ship their merchandise to the Eastern seaboard by way of the Mississippi and Spanish New Orleans far more cheaply than by sending wagon trains across the mountains. In other words, the freedom of navigation on the Mississippi was essential to their economic welfare.

Secretary Jay was aware of the West's need, but her settlers formed only a small percentage of the entire American population. So, in order to obtain the badly needed Spanish trade, he thought it preferable to let Spain close the Mississippi, reasoning that in another twenty-five years the growth of the West would be so great that her people could force Spain to open the river.

The Confederation Congress voted on the matter along sectional lines, the seven industrial states of the North approving Jay's proposal, the six agricultural states of the South opposing it. Since the vote of nine states was necessary to pass a measure, the negotiations with Spain collapsed.

American statesmen were horrified by the blind determination of Northern shipowners and manufacturers to advance their own commercial interests. General Washington, who would become the nation's first President under a new Constitution in three years, wrote to friends that he thought it imperative to "make easy the way for those settlers to the westward."

Thomas Jefferson in January, 1787, declared that an act "which abandons the navigation of the Mississippi is an act of separation between the Eastern and Western Country. . . . If the Westerners declare themselves a separate people, we are incapable of a single effort to retain them. Our citizens can never be induced, either as milita or as soldiers, to go there to cut the throats of their own brothers and sons. . . ."

The principal author of the Declaration of Independence instinctively understood his fellow Americans and believed that a rebellion was brewing in the West. But he was not alarmed. Such rebellions, he thought, were "as necessary in the political world as thunderstorms in the physical world."

Charles Pinckney, one of South Carolina's leading statesmen and a delegate to the Confederation Congress, best summed up the attitude of the West in the final hours of debate on the Jay-Gardoqui treaty. "Should the right of navigation be surrendered," he demanded of the Northern delegates, "can the Western people be blamed for immediately throwing themselves into Spanish arms for that protection and support which you have denied them? Is it not to be clearly seen, by those who will see, that the policy of Spain in thus inducing us to consent to the surrender of navigation for a time, is, that she may use it for the purpose of separating the interests of the inhabitants of the Western Country entirely from us and making it subservient to her own purposes? Will it not produce this? When once this right is ceded, no longer can the United States be viewed as the friend or parent of the New States, nor ought this nation to be considered in any light than that of their oppressors."

Franklin and Kentucky were stunned by the callous indifference of the industrial states to their interests. Their economic survival depended on their right to use the Mississippi River, and, if the waterway should be denied to their barges, they certainly would starve. Late in 1786 a rumor swept through the West that the treaty had been passed by the Confederation Congress, and, even though the report was soon proved false, John Jay was hanged in effigy in a score of frontier settlements.

It was at this critical time that Franklin began to feel completely cut off from all other parts of the United States. The states of the South, supporting North Carolina, had opposed her bid for separate statehood, and now the North was trying to choke off her only means of earning a living. A sense of despair crept over her people, and Jefferson and Pinckney were right: Franklin began to think of completely separating herself from the United States.

Kentuckians were aggravated, too, but their situation was not as hopeless as that of their neighbors. They had been guaranteed statehood, and consequently a majority preferred certain inclusion in the Union to a dubious future as a small, independent nation.

But Franklin had been given no cause to look forward to a future as an American state. The North Carolina legislature had just slammed the door again, and the prospects of statehood were as bleak as they were remote. The leaders of Franklin, including Governor Sevier, Cocke and the Campbells, began to speak openly of establishing a nation of their own, a nation that would accept friendship from anyone who offered it to them.

Their attitude was not unique, and there were many in Georgia, particularly in the new settlements that eventually would become the states of Alabama and Mississippi, who felt as they did. Kentuckians sympathized with them, and George Rogers Clark, the hero who had done more than anyone else to win the West from Great Britain, seriously considered a plan for the establishment of a separate, united nation in the West.

Nowhere in the United States was the attitude of the Franklinites regarded as treasonable. There was general disdain for the Confederation Congress, and plans already were being formulated to call together a Constitutional Convention for the purpose of providing the United States with a new, strong national government.

The major powers of Europe were keeping close watch on the deteriorating American situation. There were many in Great Britain who believed that the new nation soon would disintegrate and that the former colonies could be recovered. France, which had played such a major role in helping the United States win her independence, thought the possibility more remote, but did believe that the West, particularly the vast Mississippi Valley, might be persuaded to shift its allegiance to another union.

Spain not only concurred in this view, but took active steps to insure that Franklin and, if possible, Kentucky become affiliated with her. Gardoqui was quietly authorized by his superiors in Madrid to work toward this goal, encourage the separation of the West from the United States and spend whatever sums he deemed necessary for the purpose.

North Carolina added fuel to the fires of rebellion in Franklin. Soon after Cocke departed for home, having failed in his attempt to win separate statehood, the North Carolina legislature passed a series of acts that seemed designed to arouse the ire of the citizens of what she still considered her territory. Governor Caswell tried in vain to stem the tide and vetoed some of the measures, but the anti-Franklin majority mustered enough votes to pass the bills over his vetoes.

One of the most obnoxious to Franklinites was an act that "forever barred" Franklin's state and county officials, past, present and future, from holding public office in North Carolina. Since none had any desire to serve North Carolina, the measure was considered a personal offense.

In March, 1787, Judge Campbell, who was still recuperating from his illness, sent a letter to Governor Caswell that summed up the attitude of the new state. He wrote, in part, "The majority of the people of Franklin proclaim, with a degree of enthusiastic zeal, against a reversion to your state. Indeed, I am at a loss to conjecture whether your Assembly wished us to revert; if so, why did they treat our old, faithful officers with such contempt—officers who have suffered in the common cause, and who have been faithful in the discharge of the trust?

"Representations by a few malcontents might have been the cause of such proceedings, but surely it was an impolitic step . . . I also blame the law which passed in your Assembly, to enable the people here to hold partial elections. If it were intended to divide us and set us to massacring one another, it was well concerted, but was an ill-planned scheme if intended for the good of all.

"The people here—for I have been in public assemblies, and made it my business to collect their sentiments—dread the idea of a reversion.

"The sword of justice and vengeance will, I believe, be shortly drawn against those of this country who would overturn the laws and government of Franklin, and God only knows what will be the event. If any blood is spilt on this occasion, the act for partial elections from your country will be the cause of it; and I am bold to say the author of that act was the author of much evil."

Franklin's leaders were ready for action, and began to study the possibilities of leaving the United States, obtaining financial aid from Spain and becoming an independent nation. The initial meetings between the officials of Franklin and an emissary sent by Don Diego de Gardoqui to Jonesboro were quiet and unpublicized, but no attempt was made to conceal or disguise them in Franklin. It was Gardoqui, not Sevier and his subordinates, who wanted matters kept secret. It was obvious that the United States would have good cause to break off relations with

Spain if it became known that the minister from Madrid was trying to woo the inhabitants of American territory.

The officials of Franklin were playing a difficult and dangerous role for frontiersmen who had literally no experience in the intricacies of international diplomacy. The author of Franklin's grand design has never been revealed, so it is impossible to determine whether the credit should be given to Sevier, Cocke, Colonel Campbell or Charles Robertson, all of whom were active in the proceedings.

The basic idea was very simple. They wanted Franklin to be separated from North Carolina and admitted to the Union under its own flag. By 1787, however, it was evident that North Carolina would not budge and that the Confederation Congress lacked the authority to force the parent state to give in.

Apparently no one in Franklin had much faith in the Constitutional Convention, which would assemble in Philadelphia. The frontiersmen were disillusioned by the attitudes of both Northern and Southern states. Long accustomed to relying on no one but themselves, they wanted to create political pressure that would force their acceptance as a free and equal member of the Union.

Their audacious plan consisted of negotiating with Spain, establishing a completely independent nation of their own—with Spanish gold to help them, if necessary—and, at the appropriate time, revealing to the United States that they intended to make a treaty of alliance with Spain unless admitted to the Union as a state.

This demand, they believed, would cause so much alarm in the United States that their burning desire would be granted with no further difficulty.

In the meantime they had to tread warily, knowing they might be caught in a Spanish trap unless they guarded their freedom. So the initial conversations were vague. Franklin made no promises, but merely tried to discover how much Spain would pay them, without strings attached, if they established their own nation.

They were in no hurry to negotiate in earnest. Cocke, the Campbells and, eventually, Sevier believed there was a chance that the Constitutional Convention might set up a Federal government with sufficient authority to win their separation from North Carolina and grant them statehood. They had everything to gain and little to lose by playing for time until they found out what the Convention might accomplish. Until then they had no intention of going beyond preliminary talks with the Spaniards.

They knew that, as fighting men, they held the upper hand. The Spanish Empire, spread out through vast stretches of North and South America, suffered manpower shortages and could spare only five hundred troops to guard all of its possessions on the Mississippi. Since half of this garrison was stationed in New Orleans, only two hundred and fifty men were left to patrol almost one million square miles of wilderness. Obviously this was an impossible task, and not even the most efficient of soldiers—which the Spanish battalions were not—could accomplish it.

Sevier and Major Elholm were convinced they could subdue the Spanish forces whenever they chose, and the realistic Elholm minced no words in discussing the potentials of the situation. "The representatives of Spain," he wrote to Charles Robertson, "must continue to pay court to us, no matter how much we hold back and refuse to commit ourselves to any course of action. Although we may not be a match for the combined hordes of savages who could destroy us in a concerted action, the Indians hate the Spaniards more than they despise us, and therefore cannot be bought by Spanish gold or promises. This leaves Spain standing alone on the Mississippi, and the commanders of her battalions, even if they be dull-witted, surely realize they are totally at our mercy. Hence there is no need for us to respond quickly to the blandishments being lavished upon us."

Franklin appeared to be in a strong bargaining position, but the members of her legislature were in an unhappy, dour mood when they met at Greeneville in March, 1787. The reason for their discontent centered on Colonel John Tipton, who owned an estate on Sinking Creek in Washington County, on the outskirts of a hamlet that later became Johnson City.

Tipton, whose family would long play a distinguished and honorable role in the political and military affairs of Tennessee, was a native of Maryland who had moved to Virginia and finally had settled in the wilderness beyond the mountains. He was a man of considerable ability and great ambition.

Although he had been one of Franklin's staunchest supporters when the state had been organized, his enthusiasm cooled when Sevier had been elected Governor, a post Tipton believed he should have held. Late in 1786 he had accepted a seat in the North Carolina legislature as the representative of Washington County—the heartland of Franklin—and there had made a number of long speeches that, he claimed, represented the views of his supposed constituents. Nothing could have been more removed from the truth. Not only was he lacking in authority to speak on their behalf, but his addresses, which were larded with loyal references to the parent state, in no way expressed the attitudes of his Franklin neighbors.

Then in 1787 he had been appointed a Colonel of the North Carolina militia and had tried to muster troops in Franklin for service in the name of the mother state. This infuriated Franklinites, who twice had hanged him in effigy. His life was in serious danger. Sevier indignantly refused to assign militiamen to guard his home, and only Judge Campbell's firm intervention saved him from the violent anger of his neighbors.

The Chief Justice went to Jonesboro in April, 1787, for a precedent-setting meeting of the Superior Court. A man named George M. Clarkson was tried for murder, found guilty and hanged on April 13th; the case was the first instance of captial punishment in Franklin. Judge Campbell was afraid that Colonel Tipton might not live much longer and took the dubiously legal step of issuing a proclamation, in the name of the Superior Court, warning that anyone who did injury to Tipton would meet the fate of the executed Clarkson. So, for the present, Tipton was safe.

The Franklin legislature made strenuous efforts to strengthen the state. A delegation was sent to Nashville for the purpose of persuading the citizens of that rapidly growing city to throw in their lot with their neighbors. Two Brigadier Generals were elected, Daniel Kennedy and the indefatigably busy William Cocke, who was also made chairman of a new three-man commission that went to

New York in order to make still another application to the Confederation Congress for Franklin's admission to the Union.

Neighboring Kentucky had been encountering difficulties with the Indians of the Chickamauga tribe, who had been defeated by Colonel John Logan in a series of skirmishes, and the Cherokee were said to be increasingly restless and apprehensive. The Franklin legislature, taking no chances, ordered four hundred militiamen to active duty, even though the cost of their wages and food would place a heavy burden on the state treasury.

Resentment continued to grow over the activities of Tipton and a few others who held similar views, and there was a strong possibility that Franklin might be forced to wage a war against North Carolina. Neither the parent state nor her offspring wanted to send brother into battle against brother, and Governor Sevier, who never shirked a battle with the Indians, showed that he was an astute statesman as well as a military expert.

His aim was the avoidance of fratricidal warfare, and he sought the one man in Franklin who was respected by both the people of the new state and the citizens of North Carolina. Brigadier General Evan Shelby, a Welsh-born immigrant to the New World, had moved to the land across the mountains after service in the French and Indian War. He had served with great distinction in the Revolution and had been advanced to the rank of Brigadier General by Virginia.

A man of considerable education and high principles, Shelby had taken no part in Franklin's independence movement. He privately favored the cause of North Carolina, where he was held in great respect, but he refused to take an active role on her behalf in frontier politics. (His son, Isaac, felt no similar sense of restraint and became the first Governor of Kentucky after her admission to the Union.)

General Shelby was named to the North Carolina legislature for Washington County in 1786 and managed to walk a fine line between the opposing factions. He thanked the people of North Carolina "for the great honor you do me," but he remained at his estate in Franklin and attended no sessions of the parent state's House of Representatives.

The Franklinites looked up to him, and the few citizens of the new state who remained loyal to North Carolina regarded him, rather than Tipton, as their natural leader. So Governor Sevier demonstrated great wisdom when he sought the help of the old General.

The two men met at the home of a mutual friend, Samuel Smith, in Sullivan County and spent a full day together conferring. The result of that meeting was a remarkable document, an agreement that had the flavor of a treaty between two sovereign nations. Shelby, although he had no real right to act in the name of North Carolina, quietly assumed the authority for the purpose, and so great was his reputation that Governor Caswell and the North Carolina legislature made no attempt to repudiate the terms of the "treaty."

The agreement was brief and simple. Sevier and Shelby declared in a preamble that they sought "peace, tranquility and good decorum in the Western Country." The balance of the document was carefully designed to insure this.

One clause provided that the courts of both Franklin and

North Carolina would confine themselves, wherever possible, to dealing with criminal cases, wills, deeds and bills of sale. The courts of both would avoid defining land boundaries whenever they could do so.

The second clause was a masterpiece of joint ingenuity. It read, "The inhabitants residing within the disputed territory are at full liberty and discretion to pay their public taxes to either the state of North Carolina or the state of Franklin." Only a very few, as both men knew, would elect to pay taxes to North Carolina, but the form and spirit of amicability and justice were being observed. It would be difficult for North Carolina to complain that her rights were being abused.

The third clause was a technical one. Fugitives from Franklin justice apprehended by North Carolina would be handed over to Franklin authorities, and vice versa. It would no longer be possible for a criminal to escape unpunished by taking advantage of the feud between the states.

The agreement was limited, of course, but it was the beginning of a return to reason, a contract made by reasonable men of good faith. And, as Judge Campbell pointed out, the mere fact that North Carolina accepted the treaty was in itself a victory for Franklin, inasmuch as it meant the parent state was recognizing the sovereignty of her offspring.

But the agreement had unexpected repercussions. Stockley Donelson was disgusted with Sevier and believed he had compromised Franklin. William Cocke publicly announced that he would refuse to abide by the terms, because, he said, he could not admit that North Carolina had any authority whatever in the new state. Many others agreed with him.

Shelby, alarmed by these reactions and the possibility of violence, wrote to an old comrade, Brigadier General William Russell, who lived in the mountains of Virginia, asking for help from the Virginia militia if the situation should become worse.

But Sevier kept his head, as did Governor Caswell of North Carolina, and the malcontents on both sides of the mountains were kept under control. Unfortunately for Sevier, many of his supporters drifted away from him, and the almost unanimous desire of the people beyond the mountains for separate statehood became clouded by bitter recriminations. North Carolina, it appeared, emerged the victor in the latest development, and many men who had been loyal to Franklin wondered whether they were supporting the wrong side.

 *Chapter 7.*

THE LONG RIFLES

IN THE SPRING OF 1787 a convention was held at Greeneville. The permanent Constitution of Franklin was finally and formally adopted, and a preamble indicates the troubled attitude of the men establishing the structure of government. The Constitution would remain in force, the authors of the document declared, "until the people of said state are received into the Federal Union, or a majority of the freemen of the state of Franklin shall otherwise direct."

This statement appeared to reflect the indecision that plagued the new state, but those who were familiar with the delicate negotiations being conducted with Spain read another meaning into it. Spain was being encouraged, subtly, to accept the possibility that the citizens of Franklin might some day associate themselves with the monarchy in Madrid. At the same time, the ground was being prepared to hold the threat of total secession over the Confederation Congress if Franklin should be denied entrance into the Union.

The leaders who attended the convention were worried. Cocke, regretting his outburst of three months earlier, made a number of speeches in which he held out a hand of friendship to North Carolina. He took care to send copies of these addresses to Governor Caswell, who, in turn, assured his old friend that the antagonism of his legislature to separation would disappear. Meanwhile Governor Sevier and General Shelby exchanged solemn new promises to do everything in their joint power to keep the peace.

Like men everywhere in the United States, the frontier dwellers' hopes for the future were nurtured by the Constitutional Convention, which had convened in Philadelphia several weeks earlier. Most of the nation's prominent leaders were delegates to the assemblage, among them General Washington, Alexander Hamilton, Robert Morris, James Madison and the man held in the highest esteem by the men of the frontier, Benjamin Franklin. Statesmen of their stature could not ignore Franklin's claim for statehood nor deny the justice of her demands, the Franklinites believed, and they had no intention of antagonizing anyone until they learned whether a new form of national government might be more amenable to their aspirations.

By autumn it was clear that ratification of the new Constitution would not be accomplished overnight. Patrick Henry of Virginia, who had not been a delegate, was loud in his demands that a Bill of Rights guaranteeing personal freedoms be included in the Constitution. Men in other states held similar views, and surprising opposition to the new form of Federal government developed in many seaboard communities. Passage of the new Constitution was far from assured, and it became evident that it would take at least a year, possibly much longer, before the individual states adopted it.

Franklinites were impatient, and the explosive situation was made infinitely worse when Colonel Tipton, with a force of fifty men, attempted to seize the official records of Hawkins County and take them to North Carolina.

A rumor spread like a brush fire through the frontier lands: Tipton had captured Governor Sevier and was planning to transport him to North Carolina, where he would be placed on trial and sent to prison for life as a traitor! According to the story, Sevier was chained to a bedstead in the attic of Tipton's house.

Armed men from every part of Franklin, some in militia uniform, some in civilian buskskins, converged on the Tipton farm. Never had the wilderness dwellers responded so quickly or so energetically to a crisis. In all, more than two hundred men reached Tipton's home, while another fifteen hundred were still marching toward it. Governor Sevier would be rescued, Tipton's property would be destroyed, and Tipton himself would be put to death, preferably by hanging.

Fortunately the rumor proved to be totally baseless. Not only was Tipton innocent, but no one was more surprised than John Sevier himself. After months of ceaseless labor he had treated himself to a short holiday of a few days and had gone hunting. By accident some of the men riding toward the Tipton farm encountered him in the forest and were as surprised to see him as he was astonished to learn of their mission. Luckily he was only a few hours' ride from the Tipton house, and, borrowing a horse, he raced there at a full gallop.

He arrived just in time to prevent boodshed. The farm was surrounded, the male members of the Tipton family were bound hand and foot, guarded by a heavily armed posse, and no one was accepting the Colonel's explanation that he had no idea of Governor Sevier's whereabouts.

The Governor was greeted by a cheering throng of enthusiastic supporters, but even he had a difficult time convincing the men that Tipton had not captured him and that the whole story was totally without foundation. At last the mob dispersed, the men feeling cheated because they had been unable to vent their wrath on Tipton.

As for Colonel Tipton and his friends, they had genuine cause for indignation. It was plain that violence had been merely postponed, not averted.

Sevier, the Campbells, Cocke and Donelson, supported by Charles Robertson and Elholm, decided to make an energetic effort to preserve peace while they could, and the Governor offered the command of the Franklin militia to General Shelby. He refused, but was deeply touched by the honor and immediately thereafter resigned his commission as a Brigadier General of the North Carolina militia, a post he had held since the end of the war. Too diplomatic to cite his real reasons, he explained that he was too old for active service.

He, like the others, was afraid of bloodshed and, in an extraordinary letter to Governor Caswell of North Carolina, recommended that he be succeeded by the one man he deemed truly capable of holding the position—John Sevier!

The old General's tactful move was widely publicized in

Evan Shelby's son Isaac remained a close friend of Sevier.

Franklin and was influential in calming tempers, at least for the moment. Certainly no one was more pleased than Shelby's son, Colonel Isaac Shelby, who had been Sevier's co-commander at the Battle of King's Mountain during the Revolution. It might be noted in passing that the younger Shelby, Kentucky's first Governor, and Sevier, who eventually became Tennessee's first Governor, remained close friends until the end of their lives.

While the ferment continued to grow, Franklinites were placing at least some of their hopes for the future on still another source. Early in the spring Governor Sevier had decided to send a plea for help to the man for whom the fledgling state had been named. Reluctant to impose on Benjamin Franklin, the Governor had finally been persuaded by his friends to leave no approach neglected.

The old man, who had been acting as honorary chairman of the Constitutional Convention, finally replied on June 30, 1787, from Philadelphia, and his letter was a diplomatic masterpiece.

Sir:

I received the letter you did me the honor of writing to me the ninth of April last by the hand of Mr. Woods, who arrived here about ten days since.

You are pleased to ask my advice about the affairs of your government. I am very sensible of the honor Your Excellency and your Council thereby do me; but being in Europe when your state was formed, I am too little acquainted with the circumstances to be able to offer you any advice that may be of importance, since everything material that regards your welfare will doubtless have occurred to yourselves.

There are only two things that humanity induces me to wish you may succeed in: your accommodating your misunderstanding with the government of North Carolina by amicable means, and the avoiding an Indian war by preventing encroachments on their land. Such encroachments are the more unjustifiable, as these people in the fair way of purchase usually give very good bargains; and in one year's war with them you may suffer a loss of property and be put to an expense vastly exceeding in value what would have contented them perfectly in fairly buying the lands they can spare.

There was one of their people who was going to Congress with a complaint from the chief of the Cherokee that the N. Carolinians on the one side, and the people of your state on the other, encroach upon them daily. The Congress not being now sitting he is going back apparently dissatisfied, that our general government is not just now in a situation to render them justice, which may tend to increase ill humor in that nation.

I have no doubt of the good disposition of your government to prevent their receiving such injury, but I know the strongest governments are hardly able to restrain the disorderly people who are generally on the frontiers from excesses of various kinds; and possibly yours has not yet acquired sufficient strength for that purpose. It may be well, however, to acquaint those encroaching that the Congress will not justify them in the breach of a solemn treaty and that if they bring upon themselves an Indian war they will not be supported in it.

I am sorry my letter in answer to a former one from your state miscarried. I cannot at present lay my hands on the copy of it, but will look for it and send it at the next opportunity. I will also endeavor to inform myself more perfectly of your affairs, by inquiry and searching the records of Congress; and if anything should occur to me that I think will be useful to you, you shall hear from me thereupon.

I conclude by repeating my wish that you may amicably settle your differences with North Carolina. The inconveniences of your people attending so remote a seat of government, and the difficulty to that government in ruling so remote a people, would, I think, be powerful inducements with it to accede to any fair and reasonable proposition it may receive from you towards an accommodation.

Your Excellency's most obt. and most humble servt.

B. FRANKLIN

Franklin's advice was sensible, and his changed attitude was encouraging. Instead of side-stepping the question of separation, he suggested that the state bearing his name offer to work out a reasonable solution with North Carolina, which at least hinted that he favored independent statehood. That attitude, Sevier and his associates soon learned from other sources, was correctly reflected in the letter. America's first citizen had analyzed the feelings of the powerful men attending the Constitutional Convention and knew that, almost without exception, they were strongly in favor of granting statehood to the newly emerging regions of the West. Time favored the causes of both Kentucky and Franklin.

But the legal situation of the latter remained obscure, and the men of the frontier were hard-headed realists who had been forced, by the grim day-to-day existence they led, to believe only in action. They were impatient with delays and, more significantly, they were convinced that when danger threatened they should attack first.

Such a threat loomed in the autumn of 1787. Nashville and the other settlements far to the West, which had remained loyal to North Carolina and had refused to join Franklin, were endangered by Indian uprisings. The younger brother of Colonel James Robertson, Nashville's founder, was killed by a party of Chickamauga warriors only a short distance from his home, and it was said that the Spaniards were encouraging the Indians to make war by offering them a bounty on American scalps.

The principal fear was that the mighty Cherokee would go to war and that their allies to the south, the Creek, would join them. Schools were closed in the Nashville area, women and children remained inside their log cabins, and the men set up sentry watches.

Colonel Robertson, whose forces were inadequate to defend the settlements, wrote an anguished plea to Governor Caswell, asking for several battalions of militia.

Caswell wanted to help, but a perplexing problem made it almost impossible for him to send assistance to beleaguered Nashville. Any troops North Carolina might dispatch to the town would, of necessity, be forced to march across the territory of Franklin. The sensitive Franklinites would probably believe they were being invaded by the

parent state, and civil war would almost certainly break
out.

While Governor Caswell pondered his dilemma, the
situation in Nashville steadily and rapidly deteriorated.
The Cherokee, Colonel Robertson learned, were on the
move. At least one thousand of their warriors had left their
villages to convene deep in the forest, only forty miles
from Nashville, and it was difficult to believe their intentions were other than hostile. The Chickasaw and Creek
were already causing trouble, and small parties of warriors
from both tribes raided isolated farms.

Colonel Robertson asked Kentucky for help, but none
could be sent, the Kentuckians having mobilized for their
own self-defense. That left Nashville with only one people
to whom they could turn—the Franklinites, whom they
had spurned. Colonel Robertson swallowed his pride and
wrote an urgent letter to Governor Sevier.

"Relieve us in any manner you may judge beneficial,"
he begged. "We hope our brethren . . . in Franklin . . .
will not suffer us to be massacred by the savages without
giving us any assistance; and I candidly assure you there
never was a time in which I imagined ourselves in more
danger."

The letter ended on a note implying that Nashville might
change its mind about union with Franklin. "If you will
give us the assistance we so urgently need," Robertson said,
"I am convinced it would have the greatest tendency to
unite our counties, as our people will never forget those
who are their friends in a time of such imminent danger."

With the threat of scalping, burning and looting hanging over the heads of neighbors, John Sevier lost no time.

He called General Cocke, General Kennedy, Colonel Campbell and Major Elholm to a council of war, and within a few hours Franklin's plans were made.

Her entire militia force was organized within seventy-two hours, a remarkable achievement in an age when word of mouth was the only means of communication. Sevier also wrote to Governor George Mathews of Georgia, enclosing Robertson's appeal and suggesting that Georgia and Franklin launch an immediate, joint campaign against the Creek.

Then, not even waiting for Mathews' reply, he sent a force of five hundred men on a march toward the land of the Creek. Georgia, he felt certain, would respond favorably, and events proved him right. Governor Mathews mobilized his own militia and sent it to a rendezvous with the Franklinites.

As soon as Sevier knew the Georgians were cooperating, he personally led the bulk of his own militia, more than two thousand strong, on a march through the forest wilderness toward the remote city of Nashville and her outlying settlements. The Franklinites, all armed with the deadly long rifles the Indians had good cause to fear, marched swiftly. Every man carried his own provisions, and the frontiersmen, accustomed to hardship, halted for only a few hours each night. Those who had horses rode with the units that called themselves dragoons. Those who were on foot did not complain at the swift pace and seemed untiring.

The Indians were aware of the column's approach, Sevier making no attempt to conceal his corps' presence in the forest. Campfires burned brightly every night, and the militiamen did not try to enforce silence on the march. The Cherokee changed their minds about starting a war and quietly returned to their homes. The Chickasaw, Creek and Chickamauga also had second thoughts, and the raiding parties vanished into the deep recesses of the wilderness.

Governor Sevier won a campaign without firing a single shot. He and his men were greeted as heroes by the overjoyed residents of Nashville, who made it plain that they were disgusted with North Carolina. Robertson was equally blunt in a series of private talks he had with Sevier.

No record of those discussions was made, but the substance of what was said appeared in the subsequent correspondence of both men. Robertson revealed that the people of Nashville and the smaller settlements of what was then the far West wanted no more to do with North Carolina. A formal request had been made earlier to Kentucky, asking if the region could become a part of that Territory when it achieved independent statehood.

Franklin's energetic and immediate response to Nashville's plea for help changed the entire situation. The citizens of the city and of the smaller settlements were grateful to Franklin and wanted to prove their feelings. The best way, Robertson said, would be by means of an election; he would request a plebiscite at the earliest possible date and would ask his people to vote on the question of union with Franklin.

Sevier was elated, of course. He made it plain that Franklin would welcome her neighbors into her fold. But he was completely honest and explained that the people of Nashville might be causing themselves more problems than they solved. Franklin's own future remained clouded, and events had proved that the only friend on whom she could rely in an hour of crisis was Georgia.

The Franklin militia marched home again, and Sevier found letters waiting for him from Governor Mathews and other prominent Georgians, congratulating the men of Franklin on the firmness and speed they had demonstrated in a time of joint trouble.

Mathews volunteered to intercede with North Carolina on Franklin's behalf and to act as her champion in Congress. Mincing no words, he wrote, "It is the received opinion of the sensible part of every rank in Georgia that you will, and ought to be, as independent as the other states in the Union."

The support was encouraging, but Sevier, Judge Campbell and other leaders of Franklin knew that something concrete was needed to keep their people united. The force he had sent to the border of the Creek territory remained there, and an additional four hundred were sent to join them, with Major Elholm in overall command of the force. There was nothing like a threat of war with the Indians to unite the frontier dwellers temporarily, but Sevier recognized that unless independent statehood was soon achieved, his people would lose faith in Franklin.

Chapter 8.

DAYS OF CRISIS

THE PROPOSED CONSTITUTION of the United States drawn
up by the Convention at Philadelphia made ample provision for the admission of new states to the Federal Union.
But the delegates took no direct, positive steps to open the
doors to new states because they were not empowered to do
so. Statehood for newcomers would have to wait until the
Constitution itself was adopted by at least nine of the original thirteen states.

Most men in the West failed to understand that the Convention was not a legislative body acting in the place of the
Confederation Congress and were bitterly disappointed.
Few of the wilderness dwellers could read or write, and
even the most basic legal concepts were beyond their
grasp. Therefore they were convinced—falsely, with
great depth of feeling—that the national government had
failed them.

John Sevier now faced the most difficult situation he had yet encountered in the administration of a state that seemed no closer to its goal than it had been four years earlier. The citizens of Franklin were dissatisfied with their lot, pessimistic over the future and increasingly contemptuous of all authority.

A temporary diversion was found in an Indian war. The Creek suddenly and unexpectedly resumed their raids on a large scale, and in November, 1787, Franklin and Georgia sent joint expeditions against them. The Chickasaw asked for the right to take part in the campaign, but Sevier and Mathews felt the instinctive distrust of all Indians that was common on the frontier and, afraid the tribe might turn on them at a critical moment, rejected the offer.

Volunteers were promised tracts of land in return for their services, a Colonel receiving one thousand two hundred acres and a private being offered six hundred and forty acres. All of the land was located in territory the militia intended to take from the Creek. Franklin promised Georgia to provide almost three thousand men, and so many answered the call that the regiments were oversubscribed and two additional battalions were formed.

The men drilled together for several weeks, paraded through Jonesboro, Greeneville and smaller communities, and Franklin's troubles were forgotten. Then, only a few days before the corps was scheduled to set out for a rendezvous with the Georgians, the martial spirit of the frontiersmen was chilled by a surprising message.

The Confederation Congress, which would go out of existence when the new Federal Constitution was adopted, proved it was not quite as spineless as Americans everywhere believed. Acting swiftly and firmly in a successful attempt to avert the war, Congress appointed three commissioners to confer with the Creek and, if possible, made a new treaty with them. Pending the outcome of these discussions, Georgia and Franklin were requested to suspend their operations.

The excitement died away, the militiamen were mustered out of service, and Franklin sank back into a dangerous lethargy. Few people cared when Governor Sevier received a copy of a petition sent by the citizens of Nashville to North Carolina, demanding the right to secede from the parent state and join Franklin. The document bore hundreds of signatures, and not until years later was the significance of several names recognized.

Three young immigrants who had just arrived in Nashville were among the signers. Two, Joseph McMinn and Archibald Roane, became Governors of Tennessee. The third, Tennessee's favorite son down to the present day, became a great American military hero and then served two terms as seventh President of the United States—Andrew Jackson.

The careers of these men lay ahead, however, and by February, 1788, the frontier dwellers were so disgruntled that approximately two hundred and fifty of them offered their services to Colonel Tipton, swearing they would back him to the death in order to return the land across the mountains to the jurisdiction of North Carolina. Tipton, armed with a North Carolina warrant for the arrest of three men wanted there on criminal charges, found out that the alleged culprits were in Jonesboro and decided to march there with his little army to capture them.

At best the venture was foolishly conceived. The citizens of Jonesboro fled when Tipton and his mob advanced on the town, and the Colonel rashly leaped to the conclusion that he should occupy the place in the name of North Carolina.

Governor Sevier heard of the action at his Mount Pleasant farm on the Nolichucky River and immediately took action. He gathered a force of about one hundred and fifty men, which was joined by many others as it marched across the country.

Tipton learned of the movement, abandoned Jonesboro and returned to his own home on Sinking Creek. About fifty of his followers accompanied him, the rest discreetly dispersing. But, a battle had become inevitable.

On February 27th Sevier reached Sinking Creek and, pausing a short distance from the Tipton farm, sent an ultimatum to the Colonel: to surrender within thirty minutes or suffer the consequences of armed rebellion.

Tipton had just learned that some of his followers, had regrouped and were coming to his rescue. So, still displaying more bravado than common sense, he replied with an ultimatum of his own, demanding that Sevier surrender to him and subject himself to the laws of North Carolina.

At this juncture a small company of Tipton's men appeared on the road, headed for the farm. The Sevier men, aiming with great care, opened fire on them, killing three horses and forcing them to retreat. By now nightfall was approaching, and the Governor placed Tipton and his band under siege, surrounding the farm.

By the following morning, after spending an exceptionally chilly night in the open, the Governor's temper had cooled, and he sent another communication to his adversary. This letter was moderately worded and appealed for reason.

Tipton replied by repeating his haughty demand that Sevier surrender to him.

His arrogance so angered the Franklinites that Major Elholm, who had joined the Governor during the night, wanted to open fire on the farm buildings with several artillery pieces he had brought with him. But Sevier sensibly refused to permit a slaughter. "We'll sit here forever, if need be, and starve them out," he said.

A heavy snow began to fall around noon, and the besieged groups, mistakenly believing reinforcements were at hand, suddenly poured out of the farm buildings, firing their rifles at their foes.

Sevier, wanting no casualties, ordered his men to fire in the air. But their opponents were in earnest, and, when two of the Franklinites were wounded, Sevier could no longer control his followers. Although he repeatedly ordered them to retreat toward Jonesboro, they opened fire, killing two of Tipton's men and seriously wounding six others. Only the blinding snowstorm prevented the casualties from mounting much higher.

Sevier was convinced that Tipton was a madman and, rather than risk additional casualties in the stupid exchange, decided to spend the night in Jonesboro, muster overwhelming forces and, by sheer weight of numbers, compel Tipton to surrender.

Not until he reached Jonesboro did the Governor realize that his two young sons, James and John, Jr., as well as their cousin, also named John Sevier, all of whom had been members of the Franklin rear guard, had been captured by the Tipton men.

Colonel Tipton, returning to his farm with his prisoners, announced that he intended to hang Sevier's sons. Even his most ardent supporters were horrified and, after arguing with him at length, persuaded him to release the boys.

Governor Sevier, watching his state disintegrating, was too sick at heart to resume the action, and thereafter both sides maintained an uneasy truce. Tipton was anxious to resume the war and sent calls—fortunately in vain—to North Carolina and Virginia for troops to "destroy the insurrectionists," as he called them.

Colonel Tipton had gone too far, and North Carolina's new Governor, Samuel Johnston, repudiated him in a stern letter. Brigadier General Joseph Martin of the North Carolina militia also rebuked Tipton in a stinging letter and lectured him at length on the folly of his actions. Tipton was so thoroughly discredited, in fact, that his few remaining supporters left him. He lost all influence and was left to brood alone at his farm, a bewildered and embittered man.

Sevier immediately exchanged letters with Governor Johnston and General Martin, and all three agreed to do nothing that would cause further outbreaks. No one on either side was prosecuted, and the leaders of both Franklin and North Carolina tried to bury the unhappy affair.

But the damage was done. The Indians of the West, seeing the settlers fighting one another, tried to take advantage of the situation for their own ends. By the end of March, 1788, the Cherokee, Chickamauga and Chickasaw had gone on the warpath, killing and scalping, burning and looting. No remote dwelling or hamlet on the frontier was safe.

Sevier had to use force and, hastily mustering two regiments of volunteers, led them against the Indians. The situation was so critical that the North Carolina militia under General Martin joined the Franklinites, and the two corps fought side by side, their differences forgotten.

The campaign was short but violent. Sevier believed there was only one way to deal with Indians who broke the peace, and burned their towns to the ground, destroying their crops and showing no mercy to them in battle. The entire frontier was in a chaotic state, and settlers by the thousands abandoned their homesteads to beat a slow, if temporary retreat toward the mountains.

The Indian war created such a shambles on the frontier that it completely disrupted normal living in the wilderness settlements. Laws were not obeyed, since most law enforcement officers were in the militia. Taxes were not collected, and if the courts met to dispense justice, there is no record of their activities. The Tipton affair had been the beginning of Franklin's end, and the unrelenting fight against the Indians totally destroyed the normal fabric of society.

The final year of Franklin's existence, or, to be more precise, its last fifteen months, is shrouded in mystery. The fragments of records that have survived are contradictory and confusing, and it is impossible to determine whether Franklin as such still existed in all of the counties that had claimed allegiance to it.

There can be no doubt that it disappeared forever in June, 1789, when New Hampshire became the ninth state to ratify the Constitution and the new Federal Government of the United States came into existence. At that time North Carolina gave up her struggle to retain possession of her

Territory, and Franklin, along with the other lands of the West, was formally ceded to the United States itself.

Part of the difficulty in piecing together what happened to Franklin in its final year is the foggy status of the state's government. Governor John Sevier's term of office ended on March 1, 1788, the day after his skirmish with Colonel Tipton had concluded. During that spring he spent the better part of his time campaigning against the Indians and

The North Carolina militia joined the Franklinites against the rampaging Indians.

was similarly engaged for brief periods in the summer and autumn of that year.

He continued to use his title, however, and signed himself as "Governor, Captain-General, Commander-in-Chief and Admiral in and over the state of Franklin." Certainly there is a ring of authority in these many and dazzling offices.

However, there is no record to indicate that another

election was held in the winter or spring of 1788 or that Sevier legally succeeded himself. It can be argued that it was unnecessary to hold an election, because he had the undivided support of the people, or so his friends claimed. Nevertheless, whether he had the right to call himself Governor or sign official documents is debatable.

Judge Campbell remained Chief Justice, too, but it is difficult to determine what duties he performed during this fifteen-month period. If the Franklin courts met and trials were conducted during this time, the proceedings were not recorded. Presumably judges and juries made their decisions in a somewhat informal atmosphere. It had been difficult since the earliest days of the state to find clerks for the courts who could read and write sufficiently well to make written summaries of cases, and so it can only be guessed that the courts now dispensed with such records.

A new name appears on the list of state officials for this final period of the state's existence. Major Elholm became Franklin's Treasurer, though whether he was elected, or appointed by Sevier and other members of the hierarchy, is not known. Regardless of how he attained the position, the choice was a bad one. Although there were few men on the frontier, if any, who knew more about military affairs than Elholm, his understanding of finances was dim.

His task was complicated by the fact that Franklin no longer made its own money. Animal skins had become the medium of exchange, which meant that a crude barter system had been established, and Elholm himself admitted that he knew very little about skins and fur. "I am unable to judge the good from the bad," he confessed in a letter to an old friend in Georgia. This meant, for all practical purposes, that swindlers could pay their debts in inferior skins and the Treasurer was incapable of preventing the perpetration of fraud.

One of the clearest pictures of life in Franklin during its final months was given, a generation later, by Senator Hugh L. White of Tennessee in a speech before the United States Senate in 1838. The son of Colonel James White, who founded the city of Knoxville, he was reared in Franklin and enjoyed a distinguished career on the Tennessee bench before his election to the Senate.

In his address he told his colleagues of the pay scale used in Franklin during these last months of the state's life. The Governor received a salary of one thousand deer skins per year, and the Chief Justice was paid five hundred. The Governor's Secretary received five hundred raccoon skins, which were worth less than deer hides in the market, and the Treasurer was paid four hundred and fifty otter skins. The wages of each county clerk were three hundred beaver skins, and each member of the legislature was paid the same. Justices received one muskrat skin every time they signed a warrant, and constables were paid one mink skin for every warrant they served. Obviously mink, which would soar in price one hundred and fifty years later, was at the bottom of the late Eighteenth century scale.

Raccoon skins were used for making hats, Senator White said in his speech, and the hatters of the seaboard knew virtually nothing about pelts. Since opossum were so plentiful in Franklin that they were considered worthless, hunters quickly developed the practice of sewing raccoon tails to opossum skins and selling the furs as raccoon.

Ordinarily it would have been the duty of the Treasurer to halt this chicanery, but, Senator White said, Elholm was so ignorant in such matters that he was easily fooled by his assistants, some of whom became prosperous at the expense of the struggling state. It is small wonder that Franklin was bankrupt by the time the area was ceded to the Federal Government.

One of the principal reasons for that cession, Senator White declared, was North Carolina's inability to cope with the Indian uprisings that occurred with increasing frequency over an ever-widening area in the final months of 1788 and the first part of 1789. Not only was North Carolina unable to call up enough militiamen to deal with the threat, but she could not afford to send thousands of men on long marches many hundreds of miles from home. Consequently it was easier and simpler to hand the entire problem to the new Federal Government for solution and, in the process, relieve the burden on the North Carolina taxpayer.

During this time Franklin was forced to cope with these recurring crises alone. Georgia had her own troubles with Indians, as did Kentucky, so the Franklin wilderness dwellers had to rely on their own resources to prevent the annihilation of their families and the total destruction of their property. "Our immediate ancestors," Senator White told his fellow Senators, "comprised an unyielding band, men who periled everything for freedom's sake." He did not exaggerate.

According to his account, Sevier and the other frontier leaders realized in 1788 and 1789 that the cause of Franklin was hopeless. He said they knew, too, that the state soon would reappear under another name after it had been ceded to the new United States Government, and they were sufficiently realistic to understand that such cession was essential for reasons of both security and finance. Therefore, Senator White said, they began to use the name of Franklin less frequently and flaunt its authority less openly in order to make it easier for the members of the North Carolina legislature to hand over their possession to the Federal Government.

Many of Franklin's citizens were destitute during this last period of the state's shaky existence. Some had left their farms deep in the wilderness to take up temporary residence in the larger towns located relatively far from the Indian frontier. Others had lost everything in raids, and even those who had continued to grow crops, cut lumber and trap animals for their fur were unable to send barges down the rivers that fed into the Mississippi, because bands of warriors were waiting in ambush for the unwary.

It is surprising that spirits remained high in spite of all hazards. Remarkably few settlers left the area permanently to make their homes elsewhere, and, although the pace of immigration was reduced for the better part of a year, it did not halt. The American people, including newcomers from the British Isles and Continental Europe, refused to be discouraged in their continuing thrust into the wilderness.

 *Chapter 9.*

AN ELABORATE HOAX

THE PACE AND INTENSITY of Franklin's negotiations with Spain increased during the last fifteen months of her existence, and this relationship constitutes one of the most curious and mysterious chapters in her brief history.

The mild flirtation with Don Diego de Gardoqui and his representatives had continued down to the early spring of 1788, but until that time the authorities of Franklin engaged in no serious, substantive discussions with the Spanish minister or his subordinates. And at no time, to be sure, were Sevier and his associates actually planning to make an alliance with Spain.

The top-ranking Spanish officials in the New World had no illusions about the feelings of the frontiersmen who had made their homes in Kentucky and Franklin. Many had served in the Revolutionary War, and all, including the most recent immigrants from the Old World, were patri- otic Americans. Don Estavan Miró, the efficient, intelli- gent Governor of Spanish Louisiana, wrote many letters to Madrid stating flatly that under no circumstances would the wilderness dwellers submit to Spanish rule. Manuel de Navarro, his Intendant, or first assistant, echoed this conviction in his own reports, which were sent inde- pendently to the Minister of Foreign Affairs in Madrid.

Gardoqui, when he first came to the United States, be- lieved otherwise. He found it inconceivable that the citizens of a nation whose formal ties with Great Britain had not been severed until the signing of the peace treaty of 1783 would have strong feelings of pride in their country. It seemed even less likely to him that the immigrants com- ing to America from Europe after the Revolution cared much about their new country, and, he said in a long report to Madrid, the paupers who went out to the frontier to claim homesteads could be bought with Spanish gold.

It was noted in an earlier chapter that Eighteenth cen- tury patriotism did not resemble that of later periods. Nevertheless, men who had fought at King's Mountain and in a score of other engagements during the American Revolution in order to win their liberty had no intention of submitting to the dictates and caprices of another foreign master.

Americans, nurtured in the traditions of earliest Virginia and Massachusetts Bay since the first decades of the Seven- teenth century, were devoted to a democratic way of life. They were accustomed to electing the officials who would govern them, rewarding the efficient with new terms and dismissing the stupid, the corrupt and the bumbling from

public office. Indeed, the prospect of taking part in self-government had been one of the principal magnets that had drawn immigrants across the Atlantic Ocean and remained a powerful force in attracting newcomers.

Spain, as even the most uninformed of Americans well knew, was one of the most autocratic of all European nations. A monarchy ruled by wealthy landowners who belonged to a few noble families, Spain allowed neither her own subjects at home nor those living in her colonial posessions any real voice in the policy making or administration of their own affairs.

Hundreds of wilderness dwellers from Franklin and Kentucky had visited New Orleans, the principal city of New Spain in North America, arriving there with their barges laden with produce, furs and lumber. They had found the place exceptionally pleasant, but had been horrified and angered by the strict political controls main-

*Wilderness dwellers arrived in New Orleans with barges laden
with the produce of Franklin.*

tained by the authorities. Several hundred Spanish troops
were on garrison duty in New Orleans, and, even though
Governor Miró was an able, tolerant man by the standards
of his own nation, the Americans found his regime
harshly intolerant, narrow in its outlook and dictatorial.

The frontiersmen had returned to their homes with
wildly exaggerated tales of living conditions in New Spain.
Hence the people of Franklin and Kentucky unquestion-
ably did not believe that life under Spanish rule would be a
paradise. On the contrary, they were opposed to Spanish
officialdom and all it represented.

Don Diego de Gardoqui gradually came to understand
this feeling and, to an extent, sympathized with it. Certainly he knew that Spain would be taking on more than

she could handle if, in one way or another, she annexed or absorbed the Mississippi Valley into her American empire. He knew the people would remain independent in mind and spirit, would disobey the strict laws made for colonial subjects in Madrid and would be extraordinarily difficult to handle. A realist, he saw there were not enough Spanish troops in the New World to control such stubborn, liberty-loving people or prevent them from rebelling.

Gardoqui, Miró and Navarro were afraid of the frontiersmen and candidly admitted their feelings in their correspondence with Madrid. Deadly marksmen, the Americans were impulsive, hotheaded and ready for a fight under almost any circumstances, even when the odds were against them. As Gardoqui and his colleagues well knew, the odds were strongly in favor of the frontiersmen in their relations with Spain.

Not only had the population of the American West become greater than that of the Spanish possessions on the continent, but other factors tipped the scales, too, to give the Americans even greater advantages. In the United States every frontiersman was a citizen-soldier who not only was familiar with firearms but would use them, without hesitation, to defend his home and family.

The Spaniards in the New World were remarkably like their neighbors. Those who lived in small wilderness settlements or on farms were subjected to the same dangers and primitive living conditions that made existence so difficult for frontier Americans, and it is not surprising they had developed the same liberty-loving contempt for authority. They were disrespectful and difficult to rule and, as they proved in many crises, were inclined to ignore the dictates of the regime. In fact, in the event of a war between the United States and Spain, it was quite possible they might side with the Americans.

The residents of New Orleans were not much more reliable. Not only did the merchants, shippers and warehouse owners of the city depend on American business for their living, but personal freedom was a potent wine, and even those who proclaimed their loyalty to Spain had tasted it, found it good and wanted more. The outlook of New Orleans had become almost as American as it was Spanish, and, having been French when founded earlier in the century, the city was inclined to treat its obligations to Madrid rather lightly.

Gardoqui had followed the instructions of his Foreign

Don Diego de Gardoqui, the Spanish representative.

Ministry when he had first arrived in the United States and opened his negotiations with John Jay. His superiors had believed, and he had agreed with them, that the chances of Spain losing her huge province of Louisiana to the United States would be vastly reduced by sealing off the Mississippi River to American traffic. The furor that Jay's projected treaty with him had created convinced Gardoqui that the closing of the Mississippi would produce the opposite result: the American frontiersmen would go to war, with or without the support of their government, in order to keep the river open.

So, acting on his own initiative, the minister developed a new policy, which Miró and Navarro in New Orleans endorsed and which eventually won the approval of the Madrid Foreign Ministry. It was Gardoqui's hope that by fanning the flames of independence in Franklin and Kentucky he might lure the West away from the Unites States, encourage the two Territories to establish one or more independent nations and, finally, persuade them to make treaties that would associate them closely with Spain, perhaps going so far as to place themselves under Spanish protection.

Gardoqui had several strong weapons that would prove useful in his campaign. Knowing that few men on the American frontier were wealthy and that even the most optimistic realized years of struggle lay ahead, he planned to offer Franklin and Kentucky—once they broke away from the United States—commercial agreements that would pour the gold of Spain into the Mississippi Valley. In addition, he was not averse to bribing American officials in the West, but he failed to realize that the settlers lived by an exceptionally high moral code. Aside from General Wilkinson and a few minor officials, the wilderness dwellers contemptuously spurned his personal offers. They would accept a gift made to Franklin, but not to them as individuals.

Acting on the advice of Miró, Gardoqui also claimed that he exerted great influence over the Indian nations of the West, the Cherokee in particular, and that he could compel them to sign and abide by permanent peace treaties with the Americans. It was true that Spanish money, firearms and rum from the West Indies could send the Indian tribes on the warpath against the American settlers and that promises of bounties for scalps could increase the tempo of savage raids. But such leaders of the West as John Sevier and Isaac Shelby could not be fooled by Gardoqui's insistence that the Indians were under Spanish control.

From long experience, Sevier, Shelby and many others knew it was impossible for any outsiders to force the Indians to keep the peace. The Cherokee, Creek and Chickasaw were proud, dignified people who prized liberty as highly as the settlers did, and the notion that they would obey a Spanish order to remain peacefully at home, when new immigrants to the West were crowding them out of their hunting grounds, was too absurd to contemplate.

In the spring of 1788, when Franklin was falling apart, Gardoqui decided to increase the pace of the negotiations that had, to date, accomplished nothing. He sent a subordinate, Don Juan de Cristobal, to Franklin in the unlikely disguise of an immigrant settler. Cristobal, an elegant young grandee who had complained that New York and Philadelphia were too crude for his taste, suffered his assignment in heroic silence and delivered a private letter from his superior to Governor Sevier.

Its key paragraph read: "His Majesty is very favorably inclined to give the inhabitants of your region all the protection they may wish, be it financial, political or military. On my own part, I shall take very great pleasure in contributing on this occasion and on other occasions."

The letter was accompanied by a purse; how much money it contained is a secret the leaders of Franklin took with them to their graves. Sevier, to be sure, proceeded with great caution, as he had no desire to be branded with the false accusation that he had taken a Spanish bribe.

He call a meeting of his closest associates, among them Generals Kennedy and Cocke, the Campbells, Stockley Donelson, Charles Robertson and Major Elholm, all of them men whose honor and patriotism were above dispute. The Franklinites quickly reached several conclusions. First, the state desperately needed money to pursue its campaigns against the Indian tribes. The manufacturers of the cloth required for militia uniforms and blankets, and the foundry owners who had gunpowder and lead for sale were reluctant to exchange their wares for animal skins.

Second, the purse was an unsolicited gift. By accepting it, Franklin would not be committing herself to any specific course of action. Gardoqui had offered it freely, with no strings attached, so the Franklinites believed they could accept it without placing themselves in Spain's debt. These frontier leaders were too sophisticated to think Gardoqui would be willing to accept nothing in return for his gold, but intended to play the roles of wilderness simpletons. In other words, they were willing to let the Spaniards discover for themselves, in due time, that their investment was a waste of money.

So Sevier accepted the purse in the presence of at least a dozen associates. The money was counted openly, and that same day Major Elholm dispatched two messengers, one to New England for cloth, the other to Baltimore for munitions and supplies Franklin needed for war against the Indian tribes, a war that Sevier and others privately suspected Spain of instigating!

Meanwhile an ultra-conservative element in North Carolina was waging a bitter struggle against the adoption of the new Federal Constitution by the state, and this, combined with Gardoqui's generosity, led to one of the strangest chapters in Franklin's history.

Don Juan de Cristobal spent a day or two as Sevier's guest at his home before his return to the seaboard, and the scene was set with great care to create an impression that might bring more gold into Franklin's depleted coffers. The principal leaders of the state attended a dinner at Sevier's house and fell into a conversation that was actually staged for the Spaniard's benefit.

North Carolina, they agreed with straight faces, would reject the new Constitution, and this would mean the permanent collapse of Franklin's hopes of attaining membership in the Union. So there was no longer a choice, the frontiersmen told one another solemnly. They would call an emergency, secret session of their legislature, and Franklin would declare her complete independence as a separate nation, but would make no public announcement of her new status until a later, appropriate time.

Cristobal was completely taken in by the hoax and returned to New York elated. Gardoqui, a very shrewd man, also was fooled, in part because he knew of the opposition to the Constitution in North Carolina. It is possible he believed, wrongly, that the state actually would reject the new form of government.

His correspondence with Madrid repeatedly refers to "documents" that he enclosed, and his guarded references to them indicate they included a declaration of independence separating Franklin from the United States. Whether the leaders of Franklin prepared such documents as part of their elaborate hoax is a matter of conjecture. In fact, some historians have accepted the whole story at face value and have assumed that Franklin spent the last year of her existence as a separate, independent nation. Repeated searches of the Foreign Ministry archives and other files in Madrid, however, have failed to reveal any such documents. And if any ever existed in Franklin itself, they have never been found.

It is unlikely that Franklin ever became a sovereign nation. The governmental machinery was in a state of collapse; the treasury was empty, and paper money could no longer be printed, because the people of Franklin and elsewhere knew that such money was worthless. Campaigns against the Indians taxed Franklin's facilities to the utmost, and her militiamen were, without exception, volunteers who received neither wages nor promises of land. In brief, Franklin in 1788 was incapable of establishing herself as a nation.

Whether Gardoqui believed the story is unknown. However, he did send the unhappy Cristobal back to the frontier with a second purse. The funds it contained, like the gold in his first gift, were used completely and exclusively for the purchase of more munitions and supplies.

One letter that has been preserved in Gardoqui's files was written to him on September 12, 1788, by Sevier. In it Franklin's first citizen asked the Spanish minister to use any influence he might be able to exert in order to prevent the Choctaw, Creek and Chickasaw from joining forces with the Cherokee in a new war against Franklin. "Our women and children," Sevier declared, "will be grateful for any assistance in this regard that you might find it possible to render."

Aside from a mild, oblique reference to "our delicate situation" when mentioning Franklin's relations with North Carolina, which cannot be interpreted as a phrase with any hidden meaning, Sevier said nothing that would indicate either that Franklin had become a sovereign nation or that she had formed an alliance with Spain. It is likely he felt he had something to gain and nothing to lose by asking the Spanish minister to use his good offices with the Indians.

A copy of a second letter from Sevier to Gardoqui, translated into Spanish, also appears in the Gardoqui archives. Whether it, too, was penned on September 12th or was was written at some later date is debatable. In it the head of Franklin's beleaguered government tentatively wonders whether it might be possible for the state to obtain a strictly commercial loan from Spain in order to pursue her campaign against the Cherokee.

There is no hint of an alliance with Spain in the letter, nor is there one word that might be construed as an application for a political alliance. In fact, Sevier rather severely spelled out the terms of what he believed fair. Franklin, he said, had no funds other than "the resources and bounty of Nature." Therefore, he declared, she would be able to repay any sums advanced to her only in "fine furs, planking of exceedingly stout oak and such foodstuffs as our men will grow when they return to their homes after a surcease from the rigors of the campaign in the forests allows them the opportunity to return to their natural labors."

The loan was not made. Gardoqui indicated in a memorandum to the Foreign Ministry in Madrid that he intended to spend no more money trying to lure Franklin from the United States. "If the desires of the people dwelling in that region are granted them," he wrote, "they will forever remain citizens of the United States. They desire to attain statehood within the framework of their own government's structure, and nothing else will satisfy them. They are permanently committed to the attainment of that end."

Gardoqui had correctly judged the citizens of Franklin and was right in his assessment of their ambition.

Chapter 10.

THE END...
AND A NEW BEGINNING

FRANKLIN'S STATUS CHANGED drastically after her cession to the new United States Government. She became a part of what the new Congress designated the "Territory of the United States of America, South of the River Ohio," which was universally called the Southwest Territory.

People from the mountains to Nashville hoped and expected that John Sevier would be made Governor of the Territory, but he was too controversial a figure, having made many enemies in North Carolina, as well as among the followers of Colonel Tipton. So President Washington appointed a man acceptable to all factions, William Blount. A North Carolinian who had long sympathized with the aspirations of the Franklinites, Blount had been a member of the first Continental Congress and those succeeding it, a delegate to the Constitutional Convention and one of the leaders in North Carolina's fight to ratify the Constitution.

Resettling in what had been Franklin, he served as Governor of the Territory and Superintendent of Indian Affairs from 1790 to 1796. He became enormously popular with his new constituents, was the presiding officer of the convention that drew up the constitution for Tennessee in 1796 and subsequently served in both the United States Senate and House of Representatives.

Sevier remained the first citizen of what had been Franklin, and the Federal Government not only felt the need to recognize his past services but also to utilize his unquestioned capabilities. No one had a greater appreciation of his talents than Major General Henry Knox, the one-time bookseller who had become an artillery expert and was now Secretary of War. On the recommendation of Knox, President Washington appointed Sevier as a Brigadier General of the Army of the United States, which was being reorganized, and commander-in-chief of the Southwest Territory's armed forces.

A battalion of Federal troops was sent to Georgia and another to Kentucky. At Sevier's request he was given a full regiment of six hundred men and was empowered to call up the militia when necessary. In the next few years he fought several brief campaigns against the Indians. Most of the tribes remained relatively quiet, however, hopeful that the new United States Government would deal fairly with them and somewhat intimidated by the presence of trained, thoroughly equipped troops near their borders.

In 1791 Vermont became the fourteenth state in the Union and was followed the next year by Kentucky. By 1796 the area that had included Franklin, Nashville and the outlying settlements as far west as the Tennessee River was also ready for statehood, and the last vestiges of Franklin disappeared when, in that year, Tennessee became the sixteenth state in the Union.

The area west of the Tennessee River, as far as the Mississippi, was also claimed by Tennessee, and immigrants settled there. This region continued to be claimed by Spain, however, as a part of its province of Louisiana, and the controversy was not settled until the area had reverted to France and was sold to the United States in 1803 as part of the Louisiana Purchase.

For years after Franklin had ceased to exist, the Tennessee legislature and courts wrestled with legal questions. Were the property deeds granted by Franklin valid? Were the judgments that had been rendered by the courts of Franklin legal? For that matter, were marriage licenses granted by Franklin authorities valid? Franklin had functioned as a state, but had never been granted statehood, so the problems were difficult. They were solved, in the main, by recognition of the legality of what had been done in Franklin's name.

To the surprise of no one, John Sevier was elected the first Governor of Tennessee, serving for a two-year term and subsequently being reelected to five more terms, a record unique in the state's annals. He also served four terms as a member of the United States House of Representatives from Tennessee and was a member of several special Presidential commissions on Indian affairs.

He was an able, honest administrator, and his career was marred only by a long and almost meaningless feud with Andrew Jackson that did credit to neither man. Sevier is buried on the grounds of the courthouse at Knoxville.

Colonel Arthur Campbell retired from politics and

military life after the formation of the Southwest Territory and devoted himself to the management of his large estates. Late in life he moved to Kentucky, where he also owned considerable property. Campbell County, on the Tennessee side of the border with Kentucky, was named after him.

Judge David Campbell, his brother, was appointed a Justice of the Southwest Territory by President Washington in 1790 and served in that capacity until Tennessee achieved statehood. Thereafter he continued his distinguished career as a jurist, serving as a Justice of the Tennessee Superior Court from 1796 until 1809, when failing health forced him to retire to his plantation near the junctions of the Tennessee and Little Tennessee Rivers, where he died in 1812.

No Franklinite had a more active, diversified career than William Cocke. He became a member of the legislature of the Southwest Territory and was a founder and trustee of Blount College. A delegate to the convention that drew Tennessee's constitution, he was elected by the state's legislature as the first United States Senator from Tennessee, serving until 1797. Two years later he was elected to a full term, and served in the Senate until 1805.

In 1797 Tennessee named a new county after him. In 1809 he became a judge of the Tennessee Circuit Court and held the post for three years. In 1813 he returned to his "natural element" as a member of the Tennessee legislature.

Unable to resist a call to war, he enlisted in 1814 as a private (after having held the rank of Brigadier General!) in a volunteer regiment that campaigned against the

Seminole Indians in Florida, and later in the same year he distinguished himself as an enlisted man in General Andrew Jackson's campaign against the Creek. At that time he was sixty-six years old.

Jackson admired him greatly, and on his recommendation President Madison appointed Cocke as Agent to the Chickasaw Indians in Mississippi, where he settled and eventually became a member of the legislature. He died in 1828, having served in the legislatures of Virginia, North Carolina, Franklin, the Southwest Territory, Tennessee and Mississippi, creating a record that no other American legislator has ever equalled.

General Kennedy, who was active in the Indian campaigns conducted by North Carolina during the final year of Franklin's existence, had no desire for a life as a public official and would accept no post other than that of the clerk of the Greene County Court. He spent the rest of his days, until his death in 1802, on his large homestead near Greeneville. A quiet man who rarely demonstrated the high spirits of some of his frontier colleagues, he nevertheless had a lasting influence on Tennessee. His primary interest in life was education, and he worked incessantly to improve the school systems, first of Franklin and later of Tennessee. He was one of the founders of Martin's Academy, which later became Washington College, and also was a trustee of Greeneville College.

Major George Elholm left Franklin in 1789, when it became a Federal Territory, hoping to find a more exciting life in Georgia, where he had first settled. But Georgia was no longer a frontier, so Elholm decided it was time he settled down as a civilian. He turned to the law, and his

Sevier enlisted in Andrew Jackson's campaign against the Creeks.

mind was so agile and retentive that he was admitted to the bar after only one year of study.

John Sevier and his other comrades in Tennessee remained Elholm's closest friends. After settling in Augusta, Georgia, and establishing a law practice, he made many visits to his old colleagues. He was the first "official" visitor to Tennessee after it became a state, spent two weeks at the Governor's Mansion as the guest of John Sevier and was voted a "medal of appreciation" by the first Tennessee legislature.

The furious pace of Elholm's living took its toll. Although still a young man, he died unexpectedly in his sleep late in November, 1799. Ironically, he had often said, "I am sure I shall die in battle, probably during a cavalry charge."

Stockley Donelson, who was a member of Mrs. Andrew Jackson's large family, lost interest in politics after the disappearance of Franklin, although he served honorably in the Southwest Territory militia as a Lieutenant Colonel and was a member of Governor Blount's council of state from 1794 to 1796. He is not believed to have played an active role in the formation of the state of Tennessee.

Like his father before him, Donelson was a surveyor by profession and staked his own claim to some of the finest property in the Mississippi Valley. He demonstrated an unexpected genius for business, and his estate became the largest and most profitable individual holding in Tennessee. His plantation, on which he grew vegetables, tobacco and cotton, was also the largest horse and cattle-breeding farm in the state. In all, he owned more than five hundred thousand acres. His estate was divided among his many children, so none of his descendants ever exerted his tremendous financial influence.

The Reverend Houston returned to his native Virginia in 1789, losing interest in the frontier after the passing of Franklin. He was pastor of two churches at the same time, in the towns of Highbridge and Falling Bridge, and established a preparatory academy for boys that reputedly had the highest educational and moral standards of any school in Virginia. In 1791 he succeeded his father as a trustee of his own school, Washington College, which eventually became Washington and Lee University.

He also became a prolific writer and contributed scores of articles to newspapers and the leading magazines of the day. Rugged and healthy, like all members of the Houston family, the clergyman lived until the age of eighty-one.

General Shelby was seventy years old in 1790, when he was offered a commission as a Brigadier General in the Army of the United States, which he declined. Repeated efforts to draw him into public life in the Southwest Territory were unavailing, and he spent his last years on his large, comfortable estate near the town of Bristol, Tennessee. He died in 1794, before Tennessee became a state, but had the satisfaction of seeing his son, Isaac, elected the first Governor of Kentucky two years earlier.

Brigadier General Joseph Martin, who conducted a joint campaign against the Indians with John Sevier in 1788, hoped to be made the Governor of the Southwest Territory and solicited the support of his old friend, Patrick Henry. Although Henry sent a strong letter of recommendation to President Washington, Blount was given the post.

The disappointed Martin moved to Georgia, but remained there only a short time and then returned to his native Virginia. There Lieutenant Colonel Henry Lee, the cavalry hero of the Revolution, who had just been elected Governor, appointed him a Brigadier General of the Virginia militia, so Martin held the same high rank in the service of both North Carolina and Virginia. He spent ten years in the Virginia legislature and was a member of commissions that helped determine Virginia's boundaries with Kentucky and Tennessee.

Colonel John Tipton, who lived until 1813 and is buried on his property near what became Johnson City, Tennessee, took no active part in public life after his feud with John Sevier. Other members of his family played prominent roles in the development of Tennessee, however, and Tipton County was named after his younger brother, Jacob, who lost his life in battle against the Indians while serving under Major General Arthur St. Clair of the United States Army. The Colonel's nephew, also named John Tipton, became a distinguished United States Senator from Indiana.

The leaders of Franklin and their opponents saw innumerable changes taking place in the future state of Tennessee, most of them beginning around 1789. It is coincidental that the same year marked the inauguration of Federal control of the Southwest Territory. The population of eastern Tennessee and Nashville had grown considerably and the new inhabitants wanted some of civilization's conveniences.

The most obvious development was the building of broad, passable roads. Until 1789 travelers either used narrow trails that presented hazards to both riders and pedestrians or else cut their own paths through the wilderness. With the introduction of broad-axled carts and carriages to the region, it was essential that roads be widened, obstacles removed and holes filled in.

At the same time there was a marked improvement in private dwellings. Until approximately 1786 whipsaws, operated by hand, had been used to cut timber, so most people built log cabins rather than undertake the hard labor of cutting planks with a whipsaw. The first sawmills, using the area's plentiful water power, appeared in 1786, and in the following year two small foundries that specialized in making crude but effective iron nails were constructed. By the time the Southwest Territory was formed there were at least thirty sawmills in the region, perhaps forty, and five or six foundries.

Solidly built clapboard houses soon replaced the log cabins. New immigrants, of course, still put up one-room cabins on their homesteads until they could afford better. For the first time stone houses, schools, courthouses and churches were erected, all of them utilizing the limestone for which Tennessee would become noted.

The pioneers brought their blankets with them across the mountains, but not until 1815, at the conclusion of the War of 1812, did bolts of cloth manufactured in New England appear in quantity. Until then virtually everyone wore homespun, most of it unattractive but sturdy linsey-woolsey, which, as its name indicates, was a mixture of linen and wool.

Around 1790 sugar was sold for the first time in the general stores of the Southwest Territory. Before then sugar maples were so plentiful that families simply tapped the trees, collected the sap and made their own sugar. Town dwellers who had no opportunity to make sugar could obtain all they wanted from their rural neighbors, usually free of charge or in return for minor services.

Salt was an even more common commodity. There were deerlicks everywhere, and chunks of salt could be taken by anyone, including small children, with a minimum of effort. Only a few stores in Nashville, Greeneville and Jonesboro bothered to sell salt.

The horses of Tennessee and Kentucky were the finest to be found anywhere in the United States and were animals of great strength, stamina and speed. Breeders obtained them from the Chickasaw Indians, who, according to legend, had obtained the ancestors of the horses from early Spanish explorers and had kept the strain pure.

The story of Franklin is an exciting one—a self-made state carved out of the wilderness almost overnight by ambitious, energetic frontiersmen who refused to be halted or even slowed by obstacles that would have forced the more cautions to wait, weigh risks and proceed slowly.

Perhaps the most prominent characteristic of the Franklinites was their relentless drive. Where others would have hesitated, they pushed ahead, and in a few short years they set in motion the forces that transformed an impenetrable wilderness into one of the most advanced and cultivated regions in the entire United States, an area abounding in bustling, pleasant cities and towns, plantations and farms that grew an almost bewildering variety of crops, a state in which colleges, schools and churches sprang up by the hundreds.

The hardships and dangers faced by the Franklin

pioneers proved that the region was no fairyland, but they overcame these hazards, just as they thrust aside the obstacles that would have prevented lesser men from forming a state of their own. Franklin may have been impractical, a wild venture, but she laid the foundations for the establishment of Tennessee, and her sons, from John Sevier to the most humble frontiersman, together made a major contribution to America's rich heritage of freedom.

BIBLIOGRAPHY

Ashe, Samuel A. "Forming the State of Franklin," *North Carolina Review*, December 4, 1910; January 4, 1911.

Bailey, Edward L. *Franklin: A Forgotten American State*. New York: 1876.

Green, James R. *John Sevier: the Incomparable*. Nashville: 1892.

Kingsbury, Oliver A. "Watauga and Franklin," *Transactions of the Oneida Historical Society*, 1894, VI, 53.

Turner, Frederick J. *The Frontier in American History*. Boston: 1921.
————. *Life of John Sevier*. Boston: 1919.

Williams, Samuel C. *History of the Lost State of Franklin*. New York: 1933.

Winsor, Justin. *Narrative and Critical History of America* (Vols. II, IV, V, VI). Cambridge, Mass.: 1889.

INDEX

incorporated into Tennessee,
58
inns, 76–77
invasion of, 48–49
iron foundry established in,
72
manifesto of North Carolina,
49–53
militia of, 44, 88–89, 91, 113,
120–122
prosperity in, 68–72
religion, 75–76, 77–79
Spain's efforts toward, 100,
101–102, 110
special commissioners to
North Carolina, 90–92
taxation, 58, 68, 108, 129
treaties with Indians, 89
treaty with North Carolina,
107–109
Stewart, Thomas, 65–66, 67
Sugar, 159

Taxation, 62
North Carolina, 6–7, 15, 29,
30, 40, 58, 108
State of Franklin, 68, 108,
129
Telfair, Governor, 83, 86–87, 89
Tennessee, 125, 151
first governor of, 114
militia, 88–89
State of Franklin incorporated
into, 58

Tennessee Constitution, 11
Tipton, John, 57, 104–105
conflict with Sevier, 126–129
rumor of capturing Sevier,
112–113
Tipton, John (nephew), 157
Two-thirds rule, 60

United States Constitution, 123,
124, 129

Vermont, 2, 93, 150
Virginia, 7, 18, 26, 61, 62, 82,
94
cedes Kentucky District to
national government, 23
on invasion of State of Franklin, 48
offers services as mediator, 34
requested to cede a portion of
western territory, 13
sides with Cumberland District, 34

Washington, George, 9, 23–24,
63, 87, 97, 111, 149, 150,
152
Washington College, 153, 156
Washington and Lee University,
156
Wayne, Anthony, 87
White, Hugh L., 133–135
White, James, 11, 72, 133
Wilkinson, General, 143